More Memories
of
LUTON

The publishers would like to thank the following companies for their

support in the production of this book

Main sponsor
SKF (U.K.) Limited

Connolly Homes PLC

Kathleen and Michael Connolly Foundation

Hayward Tyler

AM Philpot (Hard Chrome) Ltd

University of Bedfordshire

First published in Great Britain by True North Books Limited
England HX3 6SN
01422 244555
www.truenorthbooks.com

ISBN 978 - 1906649791

Text, design and origination by True North Books
Printed and bound by The Charlesworth Group

More Memories
of
LUTON

CONTENTS

INTRODUCTION

Such has been the popularity of our previous book on the Luton area, that we have been encouraged to produce a new publication. Our books allow readers to walk on cobbled streets, browse in well known local shops of the period and revisit special events and occasions, without leaving the comfort of their favourite armchair.

'Change' is relentless and in some parts of the area the transformation will be more obvious than others. Luton town centre and the roads around it have changed significantly from times gone by. Some of the older and architecturally impressive buildings have retained their originality on the outside, but their uses have changed.

The title of this new book, 'More Memories of Luton', tells you all you need to know about what is captured within its pages. Turning over leaf after leaf will bring you to a treasure trove from the last century. Through the photographs and thoughtful text, the reader is taken on a ride back through the mists of time to an age when mum would nip into Woolworths and dad could buy a suit at the Fifty Shilling Tailor. We make no apologies for the fact that some of the photographs will be outside living memory because they will still be familiar to us. They may feature an event described to us by a close relative or they could feature historical landmarks such as bridges and buildings.

Whatever the view taken on the boundaries which separate 'history', 'nostalgia' or 'the present', we should all invest a little time occasionally to reflect on the past and the people and events which helped to shape life as we know it today.

Luton has always been a vibrant town, buzzing with energy, but different episodes in its life can be seen here. So, think of youthful days at the old dance hall or courting in the cinemas of old and be entertained again as we revive More Memories of Luton...Happy memories!

TEXT	STEVE AINSWORTH, BRENDAN O'NEILL
PHOTOGRAPH RESEARCH	BRENDAN O'NEILL
DESIGNER	SEAMUS MOLLOY
BUSINESS DEVELOPMENT MANAGER	STUART KIRKBY

VICTORIAN & EDWARDIAN
LUTON

This selection of early 20th century photographs of Park Square in Luton reveals an ever changing picture. The earliest, from Edwardian times shows the scene just a few short years before the arrival of the electric trams. Until very recent times trams have been thought of as dreadfully old fashioned, but what goes around comes a round – cities such as Manchester and Sheffield for example now have extensive

comparatively modern times was the ubiquitous gas lamp, examples of which are pictured here. Night life often centred around the lamps, whilst daytime activities for children included swinging on the lamps' arms or using then as makeshift cricket stumps. Though gas lamps stayed around into the 1960s they were gradually replaced over many years. Surprisingly their death knell had been sounded by the trams. Most towns were plumbed for gas at an early period, but there was no similar infrastructure to deliver the new-fangled electricity. Trams however required such a power source, and as a result electricity distribution initially followed in the wake of the tramways.

modern tramway systems. For Luton the modern age arrived in 1908. The complete system had five routes all originating at the Town Hall. The route via Park Square was George Street, Park Street and on to the depot situated opposite Bailey Street. The trams were certainly a lot cleaner than horses – as the road surface all too visibly attests. Boot scrapers by the door were not ornaments in those days but an absolute necessity. One long gone feature of everyone's lives until

Above, below and top, facing page: The New Bedford Road runs north out of Luton, parallel to the Old Bedford Road to its east. Even when these photographs were taken in the early years of the 20th century the word 'new' in the road's name was somewhat misleading: the move to improve the road towards Bedford had been enshrined in a Turnpike Act of 1727, one of the earliest such Acts in the country. It's easy to see from the obvious age of the trees that line the road that there's nothing very 'new' about the road at all. Between the two roads, old and new, lies Wardown Park. The park itself started out as a private estate owned by Richard How. Richard's son, Robert, built the first property within the park, called Bramingham Shott, which now houses the museum. In 1904 local

councillors Asher Hucklesby and Edwin Oakley purchased the property for £16,250 on behalf of Luton council.

Below: The Temperance Commercial Hotel once occupied a prominent position in George Street. The word 'temperance' referred to the fact that this was a 'dry' hotel, in other words it sold no alcohol. The idea of a pub with no beer sounds a little improbable to 21st century ears, but the temperance movement once had a vast following. It began in 1832 when Joseph Livesey founded the Preston Temperance Society whose pledge required members not to drink spirits. But Livesey pressed the issue of total abstinence and, in August 1832, he and six others first signed the pledge: "We agree to abstain from all liquors of an intoxicating quality, whether Ale, Porter, Wine, or Ardent Spirits, except as Medicines." Livesey and his colleagues became known as the 'Seven Men of Preston'. In September 1834 they formed The British Teetotal Temperance Society.

These two pictures of Chapel Street are perhaps only ten years apart. The later of the two is dated 1908. And though the older picture is from the 1890s it might almost have been the 1790s. Were there really ox-carts being driven through Luton only just beyond living memory? Well, yes there were, and here's the photographic evidence to prove it. The scene is Dickensian complete with a cast of 'characters' to provide local colour: the bent old gaffer with his walking stick, the prosperous grocer with his apron on under his jacket chatting to neighbouring storekeepers and potential customers, and the bit part players, the men and women who fill the street with life.

Meanwhile, the 1908 picture captures a tram passing along Chapel Street, quite probably the very first tram to do so. Its route was George Street, Chapel Street, Windsor Street, Hibbert Street, Ashton Road, London Road to a terminus at the junction with Tennyson Road.

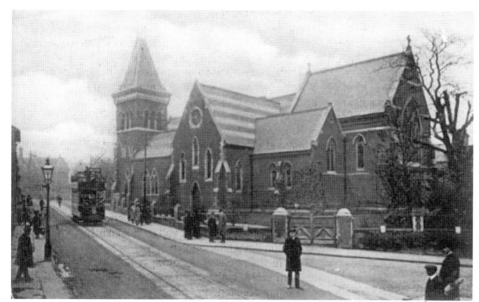

Above: This picture of Christ Church, Luton, taken around 1912 is very much a reminder of another age. Throughout most of the 20th century, right up until today, church attendance and an interest in organised religion has been on the decline. But in Victorian times interest was still strong, and church building was a significant source of work for the construction industry. A burgeoning population needed new churches to accommodate them, and wealthy men were almost queuing up to ensure than their names were entered in St Peter's big book as public benefactors. Churches were very

much a central part of community life, attendance was high, and at Sunday school even higher. It was not to everyone's taste, however. To many Sunday was blighted by shops being shut, and pubs being only allowed to open for restricted hours. For children being forced into Sunday-best clothes to visit relatives after church was a weekly torture.

Below: Funny how many of us still refer to 'steam rollers', and 'steam rolling' when such leviathans have not been used on our roads now for half a century. The only place to see one of these beasts today is at a steam rally where wonderfully cared for and restored examples are displayed for public admiration. This monster of the road is making its way up Castle Street in 1907: it must be a school day, and during school hours, since there is no crowd of fascinated small boys following the steam roller and throwing things in front of it just to see what will happen. Britain was a major exporter of steam rollers to the world, with the firm of Aveling and Porter probably being the most famous. After Aveling and Porter, the most popular were Marshall, Sons & Co., John Fowler & Co., and Wallis & Steevens.

Straw hats were a prominent feature of Wellington Street when these two photographs were taken in the early decades of the 20th century. As for the glass globes on those gas lights outside the store on the left, how long would they last today? Probably until the next Saturday night when some drunken reveller decided to wreck them. But in truth they were probably at pretty much the same level of risk of damage when they were installed; what naughty boy could resists chucking a stone at them if he thought he could get away with it? Experience is the best teacher and what seemed like a good idea at the time would turn out to be an expensive mistake. Large glass globes may have been the latest thing, but their fragility made them impractical from the very day they were installed. Few if any such features which once adorned buildings and bridge parapets all over Britain have survived into modern times.

Above: Manchester Street in Luton is pictured here just before the First World War. The Luton Corporation Tramways Order of 1905 had authorised the construction of 5 miles of tramway. The entire system opened on 21 February, 1908, and consisted mainly of single-track routes, and was Bedfordshire's only tramway. The lines radiated from the Town Hall, northwards along Manchester Street and New Bedford Road to Wardown Park; north-eastwards along Midland Road and High Town Road to Stockingstone Lane, Round Green; south-eastwards via George Street, Park Street and Bailey Street to the depot; southwards off George Street, Chapel Street, Hibbert Street and Ashton Road to London Road; and north-westwards along Upper George Street and Dunstable Road. At the end of the line the trams didn't turn round but went into 'reverse' by the simple expedient of the driver removing his handle and walking back to the identical driving position at the other end of the vehicle.

Right: This scene depicts Dunstable Road in that happy period between Queen Victoria's death in 1901 and the outbreak of the Great War in 1914. The gas lamps look as though they might be a fairly recent arrival; it's probably true in this case since the houses were not old when this photo was taken. Luton's streets had however been gas lit as far back as 1834. Prominent among Dunstable Road's early residents was Dr Oliver Smithson whose home and surgery was at 163 Dunstable Road. In 1906 he was joined by Dr Robert Daniels Bell. Soon afterwards Dr Smithson emigrated to Australia. Dr Bell's involvement with the Luton Union House, the Bute Hospital, the Children's Hospital and various Provident insurers gained him great respect. Dr Bell enlisted in the RAMC during the First World War and in 1917 was gassed in the trenches. In 1918 he was decorated at Buckingham Palace with the Military Cross for gallantry and distinguished service in the field.

Above, below and top right: The historic public water fountain which once adorned Market Hill. In these picture the fountain has already been 'upgraded' by having its original gas lantern exchanged for an ultra-modern electric light. Though intended for public use, the fountain was later fenced off, as can be seen in the top right picture, due to fears about water quality. The fountain known locally as The Pepperpot, was actually the Ames Memorial, dedicated to magistrate and landowner, Lt Col Lionel Ames. It was demolished in 1926.

lady on the far left. Although restrictive skirts first appeared in Western fashion in 1880s, the term was first used in reference to a short-lived trend of narrow skirts in around 1910-1913. The Parisian fashion designer Paul Poiret is sometimes credited with the design. To prevent tearing the skirt when women attempted to walk in them, a fetter made of braid was sometimes worn around the skirt under the knees. There was also an elasticised band available that had two connected loops, one to be worn on each leg just below the knee, underneath the skirt; this invention also kept women from taking too large a stride.

Below: At first glance this view of George Street and Corn Exchange may look Victorian. However, the car in the centre gives the game away, as does the hobble skirt worn by the

AT LEISURE

Below and right: Sir Julius Wernher purchased the Luton Hoo Estate and the Manor of Luton from Madame de Falbe around 1903. He carried out substantial renovation works to the Manor and grounds. On his death in 1912 the estate passed to Lady Ludlow.

In 1920 Lady Ludlow presented the Park to the people of Luton in memory of her son Alex Piggott Werner who was killed in action during the First World War. She unveiled the War Memorial to her son, which is located in a central position in the park, at a ceremony on 10 December, 1922, when the site was officially named Luton Hoo Memorial Park.

The original park benefited from a range of facilities, considered at the time to improve public health, including a bandstand, tearoom, glasshouses, a shelter and public toilets. Other features included pitch and putt, an ornamental rockery and a reflective garden area and promenade adjacent to the Memorial. Luton Corporation constructed the Southern and Northern entrances to the Park from Tennyson Road in 1923 at a cost of £830.

Below: These days the term 'wireless' has something to do with computers and the internet. But to these gentlemen who are all members of the Luton Wireless Society, and indeed to all the older generation, the word 'wireless' meant what today is usually referred to as radio. Wireless-telegraphy, to give it its full title, was a wonder of the age. Developed by the Irish-Italian Marconi Company, wireless telegraphy had over the course of just a few years begun to transform communications. Initially used to transmit messages by Morse code the technology had become famous when it was used to transmit distress signals from the sinking Titanic in 1912. It had also been used to send a message to the ship carrying the infamous murderer Dr Crippen, who had thought that once on the ocean he was safe from pursuit. The BBC began the world's first wireless service in 1922.

Right: Luton's outdoor municipal swimming pool pictured here in the summer of 1939 looks just the place to be on a hot day. However, things were about to get a good deal hotter. These youngsters think they haven't a care in the world. How wrong could they be? Even older folk think everything is going to be fine; hasn't the Prime Minister Mr Chamberlain been to Germany and had a stern chat with that Hitler chap? The previous summer Mr Chamberlain had indeed travelled to Munich and brought back a piece of paper signed by Herr Hitler promising 'Peace in our time'. Sadly, within weeks of this photo being taken the illusory hope of peace was ended by Hitler's invasion of Poland. War, not peace, would occupy the next six years. Happily, by the 1970s, when the baths were home to an 'It's a knockout' competition, memories of the war had begin to fade.

Below and bottom right: Luton's outdoor Municipal Swimming Pool pictured here in the summer of 1939 looks just the place to be on a hot day. Things were however about to get a good deal hotter. These youngsters think they haven't a care in the world. How wrong could one be? Even older folk think everything is going to be fine; hasn't the Prime Minister Mr Chamberlain been to Germany and had a stern chat with that Hitler chap? The previous summer Mr Chamberlain had indeed travelled to Munich and brought back a piece of paper signed by Herr Hitler

promising 'Peace in our time'. Sadly within weeks of this photo being taken the illusory hope of peace was ended by Hitler's invasion of Poland. War, not peace, would occupy the next six years. Happily by the 1970s when the baths were home to an 'It's a knockout' competition memories of the war had begin to fade.

Below: 'Alma' refers to a battle in the Crimean war. The Alma Kinema, located on the corner of Alma Street and New Bedford Road, opened on 21 December, 1929, with 'Divine Lady' starring Corrine Griffith. Designed by noted cinema architect George Coles, seating was provided in stalls and circle levels. The proscenium was 38 feet wide, and the stage 23 feet deep, with six dressing rooms. ABC closed the Alma on 28 March, 1948. It was then re-named the Alma Theatre and went over to live theatre performances presenting plays, high class variety shows, musicals and opera. Films were re-introduced in July 1954, but this use was short lived, and it was altered again to become the Cresta Ballroom. The building was demolished in July 1960, and an office block named Cresta House was built on the site. Sandy Powell MBE (1900-1982), who was appearing when this picture was taken, was a famous comedian best known for his radio work of the 1930s and for his catchphrase "Can You Hear Me, Mother?".

Below: On 17 April, 1963, the Beatles played live at the Odeon cinema in Luton. Perhaps the impressive car in the foreground of this picture belongs to one of them! The Odeon was built in 1938 with a capacity of almost 2,000 seats. The first film to be shown was 'The Drum' which starred the well-known Indian actor Sabu. In 1974, the Odeon was converted into a triple-screen cinema but television was eating into its customer base and would soon pull down the curtain on most of Luton's cinemas. The Odeon closed in 1983 and was converted into a bingo club. In 1997 its new name – The Mecca – brought controversy to the town, when objections to the name were raised on religious grounds: matters were, however, resolved amicably.

Designed by Associated British Cinemas in-house architect William R Glen, this magnificent art-deco building opened its doors for the first time on 17 October, 1938, as the 1,892 seat cinema known then as The Savoy. In 1953, The Savoy became the first cinema in the area to show a 3D film, and the first in South Beds to install Cinemascope and stereophonic sound.

The venue changed its name to ABC in 1961 before closing for around five months in 1971 when it was converted into a three-screen cinema. The cinema changed its name once again in 1987 - this time becoming the Canon cinema - before in 1996 reverting to the ABC. A rival ultra-modern multiplex cinema in the nearby Galaxy Centre opened in 1998, and two years later ABC bosses decided enough was enough. The venue screened its last film on 23 November, 2000. Today however the ABC Cinema building could be set for a facelift with the ABC Savoy Community Trust planning to restore the building to its former glory.

STREET SCENES

Above: Cowper Street takes its name from the Earls of that name. By the time this photograph was taken in 1914 Francis Thomas de Grey Cowper, 7th Earl Cowper and Lord Lieutenant of Bedfordshire had died without issue, rendering the title extinct in 1905. There are not many people about in Cowper Street on the day this picture was taken. Perhaps they too had all gone off to seek extinction themselves by rushing to sign up for the armed forces to fight Germany, a war which had just been declared. We do know that at least one resident of Cowper Street got caught up in the horrors of the First World War: George Janes, Private 79040, of the 1st/7th Battalion, Durham Light Infantry. Born and enlisted in Luton, and husband of Ada Jane Janes, he lived at 106, Cowper Street. He died on 6 September, 1918, aged 41, just two months before the war ended.

Top right: St Mary's parish church in Luton appears as the one building of any age or any great architectural merit in an area of Luton which has seen more than its share of modern development. The building consists of a west tower, chancel, nave (of five bays), north and south aisles with north and south porches attached, north and south transepts, two chapels (the Hoo chapel east of the south transept and the Wenlock chapel east of the north transept) and a north vestry. A feature of the exterior is the chequer work of flint with a contrasting stone, a feature of the north Chilterns which can also be seen at Houghton Regis and Totternhoe. The oldest part of the church is thought to date from as early as 1190. Over the course of the subsequent 900 years endless modifications have been made to its original structure.

Below: Here's Dallow Road, Luton pictured in 1906. The houses were then still almost new, and most of the residents were likely to have been the first occupants. But how times have changed: rooflines then were not garnished with television aerials and satellite dishes, nor was the road choked with parked cars. Edwardian Luton was still a place where the street was a place to congregate, where even the smallest of children could be simply pushed out of doors and told to go and play without fear of them being run over by traffic or otherwise coming to grief. These years were the 'Golden Years', jolly, plump cigar-smoking, brandy-drinking King Edward sat on the throne ruling over the greatest Empire the world had ever seen. Britain ruled the waves and nothing could go wrong. Ten years later however no doubt several of the youngsters seen here were dead victims in 'the War to End War'.

Right and below: The Free Library, often known as the Carnegie Library, occupied a site at the junction of George Street and Williamson Street, immediately north-east of the Town Halll. It was built on the site of a previous library. The Public Library, the gift of Andrew Carnegie, was opened by Whitelaw Reid, the American Ambassador, on 1 October, 1910. Mr Carnegie, who was present, expressed himself well pleased with the building; this land had cots

£12,000, which was entirely met by him. Mr Carnegie was subsequently presented with the Honorary Freedom of the Borough. Andrew Carnegie (1835-1919) was an American millionaire and philanthropist. He had been born in Scotland but emigrated to the United States with his parents as a child. Having made millions from steel he used his vast wealth to build many public libraries throughout the English-speaking world.

Below: Castle Street is pictured here in the summer of 1918. No doubt many visitors to Luton seeing the name of the street have looked hopefully for an historic castle. In 1137 Luton's Lord of the Manor built a new church. In 1139 he built a castle. The castle was, however, demolished in 1154, but not before it gave its name to Castle Street which has been with us ever since. In this scene motor vehicles have yet to make their impact on our roads. Many motor vehicles did however, exist, it's just that the majority of them were in the service of the armed forces. Three months after this picture was taken the war would end and before long surplus vehicles would begin to flood the market. The majority of them would be motor lorries, vehicles which would be snapped up by hauliers and other businesses which until then had been reliant on the most literal kind of horsepower.

Above, below and top, facing page: Edwardian Luton is pictured here at its busy best. Cars have barely begun to intrude on our roads, and instead the street is filled with pedestrians, horses and trams. No need for special pedestrian precincts when nothing travelled at more than ten or fifteen miles and hour.

In 1856 a small tower and clock was added in commemoration of the Crimean War. On Peace Day, 19th July, 1919, the Town Hall was burnt down during a riot by ex-servicemen unhappy with unemployment and other grievances.

Below: Following the destruction of the old town hall in 1919, work finally started on a replacement building in 1930; it took until 1936 to complete. The new town hall was to be a steel-framed building clad in grey Portland stone; construction used no fewer than seven million bricks. H.R.H. the Duke of Kent opened the building on 28 October, 1936. It has many typical Art Deco features, but is correctly described as neo-classical on account of the contrast between the classical and modern styles.

The original Town Hall was built in the classical style with Doric columns supporting a frieze designed by Luton architects John Williams and Sons in 1846 and cost £2,200, excluding the purchasing of the land. It was built by the Town Hall Company to hold public meetings and entertainment in the town and was only bought by Luton town council in 1874.

Demonstrating another modern style is the lady crossing the street. On 12 February, 1947, Dior launched his first fashion collection for Spring-Summer. The show was presented in the salons of the company's headquarters at 30 Avenue Montaigne, in Paris. The collection went down in fashion history as the 'New Look' after the editor-in-chief of Harper's Bazaar, Carmel Snow exclamed, 'It's such a New Look!'

town a second fair was granted each October from 1338. In time the market became a permanent feature of the town and Market Hill became the natural name for its location. Here are two scenes of Market Hill captured a generation apart; one from the late 1890s the other from the 1930s. The earlier picture has an almost 'Oliver Twist' quality, horses are the only means of transport and the clothes are from another age. The later picture, despite being some 80 years old, looks familiar to us. It may be a long time ago but things

Above and top right: By 1240 the town of Luton, then spelled Leueton, had an annual market for surrounding villages in August each year, and with the growth of the

have changed less since then than in the far shorter period which separates the two scenes.

tremendous local fundraising efforts had enabled building to begin in 1937. There would be six wards and an outpatient department. A casualty unit was essential as the first one in Luton, opened in 1933 at 'The Bute', had already proved its worth. A twin theatre unit was also opened, so that never again would there be waiting lists for surgery! There was also to be a large private wing with a theatre and a nurses' home. Local builder, H C Janes, submitted the lowest tender of £111,231 and had been awarded the contract. Queen Mary formally opened the new hospital on 14 February,

Below: The Luton and Dunstable Hospital is pictured here in 1940, the second year of the Second World War. The hospital was then just over a year old. Pre-NHS,

1939. She was accompanied by Dr John Bone, a retired general practitioner and first President of the hospital, and Miss Edith Redman, Matron.

Left: Here's Clarendon Road in Luton as it was long ago. Can you remember when it looked like this? Did you ever go into the shop on the left? If you can then you must be getting very long in the tooth. Meanwhile, we wouldn't want to be leaving an unattended bike against a wall these days. But in the 'good old days' you could leave your bike anywhere with a pound note resting on the saddle and it would never come to harm. Well, that's what some folk say, but we doubt it was ever true. The fact is that the magistrates' courts saw their daily quota of thefts, drunkenness and violence just as they do today. Times change but human nature doesn't. True there may have been less theft, but then most of us back then had far less to make it worthwhile anyone stealing.

Below: Dunstable Road was captured for posterity by a cameraman in 1946. It's a bright sunny day in the summer, as evidenced by the plethora of blinds out over the shop windows. Originally Dunstable Road was lined with Victorian houses, each with a neatly-fenced garden, but the character of the road altered with the coming of the trams in 1908; the houses were turned into shops, and their front gardens became

paved forecourts. Traffic has long been a problem in the area. In 1926, complaints were made that horses and carts were causing obstructions by stopping at a water trough at the junction of Dunstable Road and Leagrave Road. In the following years the junction was covered by constables on point duty. Today, the area has changed yet again, but in 1946 when this peaceful scene was captured change was not on people's minds, just relief that the war was over and normal life could at last resume.

Above: The Cornmarket roundabout is pictured here in the late 1950s. The volume of traffic is remarkable for still being so thin that pedestrians can happily wonder across the road at will with little fear of being run over. On the left is Halfords. The Halford company was founded by Frederick Rushbrooke in Birmingham in 1892 as a wholesale ironmongery. In 1902, Rushbrooke moved to a store on Halford Street, in Leicester, after which the company was named, and started selling cycling goods from there. The company opened its 200th store in 1931 and purchased the Birmingham Bicycle Company in 1945. In 1968, it opened its 300th store. Today, it has 10,000 employees and a turnover of over £850 million. When this photo was taken, however, Halford's was still an unpretentious operation, with out of town superstores still unimagined. Simple cycles and cycle accessories were the order of the day, and, as can be seen, the Luton branch of Halford's certainly had no shortage of potential customers.

THE WAR YEARS

Right, below and top, facing page: The First World War was already a year old when these photographs of soldiers were taken at Biscot camp outside Luton. Biscot was home to the Royal Field Artillery training school, and no doubt this is the unit these young servicemen belong to. Much to their surprise the war which had begun at the end of the previous summer was still going strong. 'It'll all be over by Christmas' had been the general consensus the previous year, and so to avoid missing out on the fun hundreds of thousands of young men had signed up at once, at the very outbreak of the war. Alas it was not over by Christmas 1914, nor 1915, 1916 or 1917. Nor, as these keen young soldiers would discover all too soon, was war 'fun'. Those who survived the horrors of the Somme and other battlefields would never imagine war to be fun again.

Below: Arthur Edmund Fisher was, despite his piscatorial name, a butcher. His premises were at 25, George Street in Luton. The notes that accompany this photograph tell us only that it was taken in 1918 and that it features the aforementioned Mr Fisher – and a tank! Who the others may be we can only guess. But we do know about the tank: in 1918 six Mark IV male tanks toured the towns and cities of England, Scotland and Wales to promote the sale of War Bonds and War Savings Certificates. A 'tank bank' would arrive with great fanfare. Local dignitaries and celebrities would greet the tank and speeches would often be made from its top. The tank would be accompanied by soldiers and artillery guns, sometimes an aeroplane would drop pamphlets over the town or city before the tank's appearance exhorting people to invest. The tank would usually put on a show for the crowds in order to demonstrate its capabilities. Towns and cities would have fund raising target they tried to meet, the amount raised in each town was reported in the national press thus ensuring a strong element of competition.

Above: Quite why the army should set up a field kitchen in Stopsely in 1914 is not recorded. Perhaps they wanted to attract recruits with the offer of free food, though in 1914 such incentives were not necessary. It was Napoleon Bonaparte who first observed that 'An army marches on its stomach'. Exactly 99 years after Napoleon's defeat at Waterloo these army cooks seem to have learned that particular French lesson. Surprisingly, however, the Army Catering Corps (ACC), responsible for the feeding of all Army units today was originally formed only in March, 1941, as part of the Royal Army Service Corps, and only became a corps in its own right in 1965. In 1993, as part of the Options for Change defence review, it was amalgamated into the Royal Logistic Corps.

Right: In 1918 the D Battery vaulting team of the Royal Field Artillery are posing for a victory photograph at their base at Biscot camp where they have just won first prize at what they dubbed the Luton Gymkhana. Sadly, we will probably never know who these riders were: The RFA was one of the largest units in the British Army, and the designation 'D Battery' could have been a gun battery belonging to any one of a large number of the RFA's brigades. The RFA served in every theatre of war, not just in France but also in Mesopotamia and even further afield. The gymkhana is a sad reminder that it was not just millions of men who served and died in the First World War but also thousands of horses.

Left: The British Legion (since 1971 the Royal British legion) was founded in 1921 as a voice for the ex-Service community as a merger of four organisations: the Comrades of the Great War, the National Association of Discharged Sailors and Soldiers, the National Federation of Discharged and Demobilized Sailors and Soldiers and the Officers' Association. This photo from 1918 shows members of one local soldiers' demobilisation organisation set up to help discharged servicemen find homes, work and obtain any pensions they might be due. During the course of war many thousands of men were discharged due to injuries received. Millions of men, however, served in the forces, and during 1919 most of them finally arrived back in Britain in need of jobs, and the 'homes fit for heroes' that the government had promised them for their efforts.

The United Kingdom declared war on Germany on Tuesday 4 August, 1914, following an 'unsatisfactory reply' to the British ultimatum to Germany that Belgium must be kept neutral. The 1/5th Territorial Battalion of the South Staffs were in Walsall earlier in August 1914. Part of the Staffordshire Brigade in the North Midland Division, they then billeted in the Luton area, and in November 1914 went on to Bishops Stortford. They landed at Le Havre on 3 March, 1915. In May 1915 the formation became the 137th Brigade, 46th (North Midland) Division and in January 1916 they moved to Egypt, returning to France next month. These photos show the soldiers doing their washing on Wednesday 19 August, 1914. On the same day the USA declared its neutrality, before later joining the war effort.

Left: During the Second World War thousands of young women helped the war effort in countless capacities. These young Luton ladies are members of the Women's Land Army. First created during the First World War to work in agriculture, replacing men called up to the military, women who worked for the WLA were commonly known as Land Girls. In June 1939, as the prospect of war became increasingly likely, the government wanted to increase the amount of food grown in Britain. In order to do so, more help was needed on the farms, and so the government revived the Women's Land Army. At first it asked for volunteers. This was supplemented by conscription, so that by 1944 it had over 80,000 members. Though under the Ministry of Agriculture and Fisheries, the WLA was given an honorary head - Lady Denman. The WLA lasted until its official disbandment on 21 October, 1950.

Bottom left and below: It was on 15 October, 1940, when a single German plane was seen over Luton in broad daylight, just before midday. A number of onlookers witnessed the plane drooping a large bomb as the sirens let out their chilling shriek. The factories and houses in Old Bedford Road and Limbury Road were badly damaged, as can be seen in these images. As it was just before noon the impact on the hat factories in Old Bedford Road was devastating as everyone, mostly women and girls, were still at work. W O Scales & Co were worst hit, with 13 killed and 35 injured. Machines were blown from the factory through the air into nearby gardens with material and ribbons hanging grotesquely from the trees. Luckily, many local children had heeded the sirens and found a safe haven in the air raid shelters below the playground at Old Bedford Road School.

SKF - A Century of Progress

SKF (U.K.) Limited based, in Sundon Park Road, Luton is one the town's most important employers. Today, the SKF Group is the leading global designer and manufacturer of industrial and automotive engineered solutions in the areas comprising bearings, seals, mechatronics, services and lubrication systems. The Group's product and technical expertise is focused towards integrated, sustainable solutions that can offer breakthroughs in friction reduction and energy efficiency, and increased equipment life and reliability. SKF solutions can be found in everything from advanced windmills for clean power generation to low-friction car drivetrain bearings and seals that increase fuel efficiency.

SKF is short for 'Svenska Kullagerfabriken' – 'Swedish ball bearing makers'. It was in 1911 that SKF's first factory outside Sweden was constructed in Luton.

The invention of the self-aligning ball bearing in 1907 by Sven Wingquist saw the birth of SKF. Wingquist was working as a maintenance supervisor at a textile factory in Gothenburg, Sweden, at the time and designed a solution to a tricky engineering problem. The textile factory was built on ground largely composed of clay, meaning that the foundation was unstable, causing the building to move, and the bearings that were used to transfer power to the textile machines to overheat.

Wingquist's self-aligning ball bearing not only dealt with the particular problems of misalignment in equipment within the textile industry, but it also offered other industries the opportunity to use a component that required less energy and lubrication, while at the same time providing greater precision, higher speeds and less maintenance.

The Skefko Ball Bearing Company Limited, as it was then known, entered the UK market, opening offices in Lower Regent Street, London, on 7 February, 1910. Three acres of land were bought at Leagrave Road in Luton, and on 10 November of the same year the construction of SKF's first purpose-built production plant outside of Sweden began.

With the 1,440 sq m building complete, production at the Luton factory began on 17 June, 1911, with 150 employees. Output after the first year averaged 180 bearings per day of Sven Wingquist's original bearing design.

In 1912, the administrative and commercial offices were moved from London to Luton. In 1916, to meet the increased demand for bearings during the First World War, it was decided to double the size of the Luton factory, enlarge the stores, and add the

Above: Founder, Sven Wingquist. **Left and below:** *The SKF Luton factory in 1911 and in 1916 by which time it had doubled in size.*

main office block, thereby multiplying the total floor area by more than eight times.

By the end of the Great War in 1918, the now 775 employees at the factory doubled the 1914 production figures with a monthly output of 24,000 bearings; that figure continued to increase in the following years. Indeed, across the globe SKF had, by this time, already experienced significant growth and, in total, had an impressive 12 factories, sales representatives in 100 countries and 12,000 employees.

In the UK, 1919 saw the opening of an export sales department, and in Birmingham, the first regional sales office. Production went from strength to strength and by the end of the year the weekly output of bearings in Luton had reached approximately 20,000 units.

Demand for their innovative bearings grew rapidly and in order to accommodate the needs of customers, by the end of 1921 further branch offices were established in Leeds, Glasgow, Manchester, Newcastle, Sheffield, Bristol and Belfast.

Over the next few years the range of products manufactured at the Luton factory was extended, with tapered roller bearings being produced for the first time at the site in 1922, and cylindrical roller bearings being made there from 1923.

However, it was not only the product range that grew, but also the workforce: the number of employees at Luton hit the 1,000 mark in 1924.

The arrival of SKF in Luton was followed by Electrolux in 1926, marking the firm establishment of a Swedish presence in the town. In fact, Luton's twin town in Sweden is Eskilstuna whose biggest employer is, rather appropriately, the Volvo-BM Group.

It was, in fact, SKF that founded the Volvo car company in 1927, producing the Jakob car, which incorporated some of SKF's earliest automotive bearings.

In 1933, a new plant was added to increase the capacity for production of tapered roller bearings as well as cylindrical roller bearings, whilst the number of employees at Luton rose to over 2,000 for the first time. In 1936, with a view to further expansion, 44 acres of land were purchased at Sundon, a few miles north of Luton town centre.

Just before the outbreak of the Second World War in 1939 extensions were completed to the Leagrave Road factory.

Above: SKF workers in the early years. Left: The Assembly Department in 1914. Mr. W.S. Braine is standing with his hand on some rings. Below: SKF's B.J. Ward with H.R.H Prince of Wales at the company's exhibition stand in Olympia, 1920.

Later the same year, the bar-turning plant was erected and, by Christmas, the ball and ancillary plant was in full production, employing 250 people.

During October 1942, a wartime record was reached, with nearly a quarter of a million bearings leaving the despatch bays each week.

Some 400 of SKF's employees saw active service with the armed forces during the war, 34 of whom sadly lost their lives in the service of their country. Following the end of the war, many wartime contracts naturally came to an end, causing some dislocation of production at Luton. However, the first stage of a major expansion plan was started in anticipation of the demands of factories returning to peacetime production.

As a precaution against air attack, elaborate camouflage was added in the form of a fake road built over the main entrance and factory building giving the illusion of a suburban avenue when viewed from above. Being vital to the war effort, there was a dramatic increase in the demand for bearings and, as a result, the workforce had increased to more than 3,000 by 1941.

Rather than keep all the activity concentrated at one spot, and so become vulnerable to the risk of total loss through bombing, it was decided in 1942 to setup a ball production plant at the new Sundon site.

The Company started transferring employees from the Leagrave Road site to the Sundon plant in 1948, and the new roller factory, along with its large bearings and heat treatment department came into production. By the end of the 1940s branch offices had also been opened in Leicester, Cardiff, Aberdeen, Nottingham and Dublin.

Considerable investments were made in the post war years.

Top left and above left: Women wartime workers at the Sundon site. *Below:* Extension work on the Sundon site in 1946. *Above:* A picture of the Queen adorns the SKF building to celebrate the Coronation in 1953.

By the end of 1951 around £2 million had been spent extending and improving manufacturing facilities.

By 1955, the largest single expansion in the history of Skefko began, including new roller bearing facilities and new buildings for light turning to allow for the development of the automatics department, a boiler house, a new electrical sub-station and a new canteen and social club with a landmark 75 feet tower. Finally, the new ball bearing factory at Sundon was completed in August of the same year.

Over the fifteen years leading up to the celebration of the firm's Golden Jubilee in 1960 there was a steady transition of processes and workforce from Leagrave Road to the present Sundon Park Road premises.

That same year the company acquired the Sheffield Twist Drill and Steel Company, as it was called at the time, before it became SKF and Dormer Tools (Sheffield) Limited. The company was later known as Dormer Tools following a management buy-out during the early 1990s.

Production continued at the Leagrave site until 1977 when all operations were centralised at Sundon, which would become the company's UK headquarters. The manufacture of bearings in Scotland ceased at Irvine in 1979.

In the 1980s changes were made to the business structure in order to take advantage of the new business opportunities for non-bearing related products, allowing SKF to focus more closely on customers' requirements.

Above: The new canteen and social centre after the largest single expansion in Skefko's history, 1955. Left: At work in the 1960s. Below: His Majesty King Carl Gustaf XVI's visit to the Sundon Park Road site in 1975

There was also further UK expansion with the opening of a new factory in Irvine, Ayrshire. The foundation stone of the new factory was laid in 1961 and by Christmas of the same year building works were completed and the transfer of the cages and cast iron departments from Sundon had begun. Over the next few years this new factory in Scotland was extended to enable the production of rings for tapered roller bearings and the assembly of these bearings to be carried out at the site by 1964. Rapidly increasing demands for ball bearing water pump spindles saw new lines set-up at Irvine in 1972.

Skefko changed its name in 1973 to that which is it known by today: SKF (U.K.) Limited.

In 1975, His Majesty King Carl Gustaf XVI visited the Sundon Park Road site at the beginning of a private visit to Swedish industry in Britain.

In 2000, DI (Diagnostic Instruments), located in Livingston, Scotland, was acquired. SKF Condition Monitoring Centre - Livingston as it is now known - designs, develops and manufactures mobile industrial computers and application-specific data collectors and analysers in the noise and vibration measuring field.

Two years later SKF acquired the NSK aerospace factory located in Stonehouse, Gloucestershire.

SKF Engineering Products Division was established early in the decade, whilst a new subsidiary SKF (U.K.) Service Limited, was formed on 1 September, 1987.

In 1988, the Group acquired the British company AMPEP plc, which was involved in the design and manufacture of self-lubricating PTFE and glass fibre-lined plain bearings for high technology aerospace and industrial applications.

SKF sponsored the first wheeled vehicle ever to travel faster than the speed of sound in 1996. Called the Thrust SSC, this groundbreaking machine was equipped with twin Rolls-Royce jet engines and achieved Mach1 by reaching 764 mph or 1,222 km/h. Naturally SKF bearings were used in the critical applications such as wheels, steering, gearbox and suspension.

On 1 April, 1997, the Luton-based firm became the first company in the SKF Group, and the first major bearing manufacturer worldwide, to achieve certification to the new environmental management standard ISO 14001.

The last acquisition of the 20th century was that of DEI (Development Engineering Consultancy) in 1999, an international maintenance engineering consultancy, based in Aberdeen. DEI had started life in 1981, serving the needs of the North Sea oil and gas industry.

A number of other strategic acquisitions took place during the early years of the new millennium.

In 2006, SNFA SAS, a leading manufacturer of super-precision bearings for aerospace and machine tool applications, was acquired together with Economos, the global market leader for customised, engineered sealing solutions: both helped to strengthen SKF's business platforms still further. In particular. Economos seals are present in virtually every type of fluid power application, and in many parts of the process sector from oil and gas to food and beverages.

This company currently has a network of 11 regional seal manufacturing centres across the UK. The network is backed by a dedicated research, development and manufacturing centre at the Economos headquarters in Austria, from where SKF provide high volume production facilities.

Top left: SKF's Irvine site in the 1970s. Top right: An SKF outdoor exhibition, 1970. Left: The Falkirk Wheel for which SKF supplied an innovative slewing bearing solution in 2001. Above: At work on a SKF spherical roller bearing.

Today, the Sundon factory produces spherical and CARB toroidal roller bearings for use in heavy industrial applications, such as pulp and paper, metals, construction and quarrying. The Company also offer a range of support services from Luton, including machine tool spindle repairs, and the refurbishment of railway tapered bearing units (TBUs).

Along with another 18 locations around Britain, SKF's UK engineering base has always played an important role in the overall success of the Company. Even during economic recession it has still managed to maintain a strong level of output, which the company believes will grow in the coming years as the pace of global recovery picks up. As a result SKF anticipates continued investment and development of its UK manufacturing operations, giving the company a firm foundation for another century of success in Great Britain.

Furthermore, SKF gained significant contracts to provide products and support to some truly momentous applications. For example, the firm supplied an innovative slewing bearing solution for the Falkirk Wheel, the giant rotating boat lift that is the centrepiece of the Millennium Link, a £78 million project led by British Waterways, which reconnected the Forth and Clyde Canal, and the Union Canal between Glasgow and Edinburgh. SKF also supplied four huge spherical roller bearings and cast steel housings for one of the world's largest deep-water pipeline laying ships, CSO Deep Blue. The bearings support two 770 tonne reels, each carrying 2,500 tonnes of steel pipe of up to 400 mm diameter, around a hub 20 m in diameter.

Top left: Work in the environment, part of the SKF Care scheme. *Above:* BeyondZero is the SKF strategy to have a positive impact on the environment. *Left:* Upgraded SKF Explorer self-aligning roller bearings. *Below:* Managing Director Sharon Smith cuts the cake for SKF Luton's centenary exhibition opening, 2011.

From its roots in an unstable Swedish textiles factory, SKF has grown from a designer, manufacturer and supplier of bearings into a provider of a diverse range of knowledge-based engineering solutions, combining evolution with a constant commitment to customers' needs and to core company values of innovation and quality. SKF is now the largest bearing manufacturer in the world, employing some 46,000 people, with around 140 manufacturing and operational sites in 32 countries.

SKF has developed a guiding principle for everyone at SKF, called SKF Care. It has four dimensions – Business Care, ensuring it has a strong financial performance and delivers the right returns for its shareholders; Environmental Care, reducing any negative impact on the environment; Employee Care, having a safe working environment and improving the health and education of employees; and Community Care, playing an active role in the communities in which the company operates.

EVENTS & OCCASIONS

I t's 5 June, 1915, and the 5th Battalion of the Bedforshire Regiment are parading through Luton town centre on their way to war. Crowds line the street to cheer our brave lads on their way. No doubt many felt like heroes already and sported happy smiles at the thought of the adventures ahead and the stories they would one day be able to tell their sweethearts, and perhaps their grandchildren. Those who survived the next few years would have a tale to tell, though many chose never to tell it. For theses men their next port of call was Gallipoli. The Gallipoli Campaign, also known as the Dardanelles Campaign, or in Turkish the Battle of Çanakkale, took place at the peninsula of Gallipoli in the Ottoman Empire (now Gelibolu in modern day Turkey) between 25th April 1915 and 9th January 1916. During the ill-fated campaign the British and Empire forces suffered 489,000 casualties.

Above: The 5th Territorial battalion of the Bedfordshire Regiment was formed in 1860. In 1900, men from all volunteer battalions of the Bedfordshire Regiment served in the 'Volunteer Service (Foreign)' unit with the 2nd Regular Battalion, The Bedfordshire Regiment in the Boer Wars in South Africa. Among these volunteers was a solicitor and rising second lieutenant from Luton called Edgar William Brighten, who would become the Battalion C.O. and lead them throughout the Great War, later going onto command a regular battalion between the two world wars. This photograph taken outside Luton Town hall in 1902 is a welcome home event for Luton's soldiers who had until, recently been serving in South Africa in the second Boer War which had just ended, and in which over 7,000 British servicemen had been killed in action and 13,000 died from disease.

Right and top right: The burnt out remains of Luton's Town Hall pictured here in July, 1919, are a timely reminder that riots are not just a 21st century phenomenon. On the ironically named 'Peace' Day, 19 July, 1919, the Town Hall was burnt down during a riot by ex-servicemen unhappy with the way the Town Council was managing the event. The riot began after members of the council arrived to read out the King's peace proclamation. The crowd loudly expressed its disapproval. Protesters broke through the police line. A number of violent clashes took place, with the Town Hall being stormed and eventually set on fire. Many valuable documents relating to local history were lost, not least a Papal Bull, sent by Pope Adrian IV to the vicar of Shefford in the 12th century. Rioters broke into Farmers Music Shop and dragged pianos into the streets for dancing and singing, not least including ironically 'Keep the home fires burning'. The Mayor at the time, Henry Impey, never returned.

This parade along George Steet in Luton took place in 1932. At the head of the procession is the town's Mace Bearer followed by the new Mayor, George Wistow Walker, the Headmaster of Leagrave School in 1895, who was mayor in 1932 and 1933. Our researchers have, however, been unable to determine exactly what this procession was for. Was it the mayor's inauguration parade perhaps? Surely it wasn't a march to celebrate the demise of Luton's trams, which made their final journey in 1932? And we somehow doubt that it was a special event to mark the invention of the Anglepoise lamp or the appearance of the Mars Bar, both of which made their debut in 1932!

Below: Flags and bunting were out in 2012 to mark the Diamond Jubilee of Her Majesty Queen Elizabeth II. For these shoppers in Luton in 1953, however, the idea that the new monarch would still be going strong sixty years after she acceded to the throne the previous year was probably not a thought that was occupying their minds. The bunting has been put out to celebrate the Coronation of the new Queen, and the New Elizabethan Age it heralded. The coronation of the 26-year-old Queen was held on 2 June, 1953, more than a year after her accession on the death of her father. The event in many ways marked the divide between 'the olden days' and 'modern times'. Televisions were sold in their tens of thousands so people could watch the coronation in the comfort of their own homes. And although post-war austerity still persisted, life for almost everyone would get better each year for many years to come.

Right: This looks a bit different from the 2012 Olympic torch relay. No teams of security guards running alongside. The two runners are pictured here in Manchester Street on a rainy day in October 1953. But why was this torch being carried through Luton five years after the 1948 London Olympics, and the year after the 1952 Helsinki Games? Had the pair of athletes taken a wrong turn somewhere and got lost on their way through Bedfordshire? The Tuesday

Pictorial, which was then a sister paper of the Luton News, reported that the event was a charity run by Loughborough College students and not in fact linked to any particular Olympic Games. The photo shows the torch being passed between relay runners outside the old Luton News building on the corner of Manchester Street and Alma Street.

Right: The opening of a new library in Luton was one of the reasons the Queen and Prince Phillip visited the town on a very wet day on 2 November, 1962. They were greeted by the Lord Lieutenant of Bedfordshire, Major Simon Whitbread, and the Queen, carrying her own umbrella, Territorial Army's First Battalion Bedfordshire and Hertfordshire Regiment. A visit to the newly opened library was next, with the royal couple meeting local people and dignitaries including Borough Librarian, Frank Gardner and Borough Architect, Mervyn Blackman. Luton Girls Choir provided the light entertainment with a short concert to end the day.

Above: Another innovative health care product developed by Huntleigh Heathcare of Luton was the world famous Nimbus dynamic flotation system for patient support. It was a mattress providing optimum pressure relief and comfort for patients or more simply put, it stops patients getting bed-sores. Obviously far more than a comfy mattress, it had automatically adjustable weight, size and position controls, separate sections for each main part of the body and sophisticated alarm and filtration systems to protect against infection. Here we see Jimmy Saville with his ever present large cigar and what looks like a glass of wine, trying out the Nimbus at its launch in Stoke Mandeville Hospital in 1989, no doubt using his catchphrase " Now then, now then, now then".

Right: It seems that incidents of DVT or deep vein thrombosis, have only become prominent in recent years due to the increased number of long haul flights taken by ordinary people. But not so, as we see from this photograph of Margaret Thatcher visiting a school in Luton in 1978. The image shows a device manufactured by one of Luton's prominent businesses, Flowtron-Aire Limited, who developed it to reduce the incidence of DVT's in those who were immobilised for any reason such as surgery or a long term disability. DVT at the time killed almost as many people as died in road accidents. The idea came from a mountaineer, Dr JP Flug and extension of the inflatable splint concept. Rolf Schild of Flowtron was introduced to this and developed a device using an air pump applying intermittent pressure through 'giant' air

filled plastic 'boots' and 'sleeves', preventing the blood from clotting. The importance of the device is shown by the visit of Mrs Thatcher shortly before her election as Britain's first women Prime Minister in 1979.

Above: What? PG Tips for 7½ p. At prices like that you know you've found a real bargain or that this photograph was taken a very long time ago. Four decades ago, in 1973, these happy shoppers were part of the celebrations which marked the opening of a new Tesco store associated with Luton's recently completed Arndale Centre. The company was founded in 1919 by Jack Cohen as a group of market stalls. The Tesco name first appeared in 1924, after Cohen purchased a shipment of tea from T. E. Stockwell and combined those initials with the first two letters of his surname. The very first Tesco store opened in 1929 in Burnt Oak, Middlesex. The business expanded rapidly, and by 1939 there were over 100 Tesco stores across the country: today there are over 6,000.

ON THE BEAT

Above: Cheapside in 1908 was almost free of any traffic apart from the handcart further down the street, but the pedestrians still needed to be controlled. The bobby in the centre of the picture seems to be posing for the photographer, but maybe he is checking to make sure that nothing untoward is going on. The young girl to the right in the white smock is probably running an errand for one of the shopkeepers, but this may have been the first time she had seen a man in a street with a large box on a tripod and his head under a cloth cover. She was obviously intrigued by the scene but no doubt was soon on her way.

Top right: As many people say 'there's nothing new on this earth' and that applies to the police force who look after Luton. In 1922, the boom after the war was at an end and the country was in real financial difficulty with cuts to public expenditure and spending on the police service suffered as a result. Forces had to make cuts by five percent, this was done by freezing recruitment and cutting officers wages and allowances. By June, the number of officers had been reduced from 127 to 123. The Chief Constable at the time, Colonel Stevens was concerned at these cuts at a time of growing demand on the police and said "The greatly increased amount of motor traffic now necessitates constables being placed on point duty at various dangerous crossings to prevent serious accidents. Police supervision is also most necessary to check dangerous driving." In 1923, the house purchase programme was suspended (basic police stations where an officer lived). And the annual issue of uniform was cancelled. It was only by 1925 that the recession eased and more funding became available. The bicycles enabled the police to cover more ground and respond quickly to reported incidents, without the need for expensive police cars. We also see police on bikes today and for the same reasons but possibly the added speed though today's heavy traffic is a help

Right: Luton police had to attend a major incident which occurred at the Kempston Flower Show on 3rd August 1926 when five people were killed in a tragic accident at this local event. The balloon, one of Spencer & Sons captive balloons, had been one of the attractions, taking visitors high into the air, about 600 feet, to admire the surrounding countryside. The balloon was attached to a

thick rope, which wound onto the roller of a motor winch on the ground. The accident occurred after a dozen or so trips that morning. When descending, the rope became fouled in a tree, the pilots then asked a number of people below to take the rope and try to pull the balloon down. However, the wind was strong and a number of men were lifted into the air. Suddenly a sharp crack was heard and the netting which held the basket broke, quickly followed by the basket itself breaking away and falling 100 feet to the ground. The pilot and one passenger were killed instantly. The police attended the three other casualties. However, one died on the way to hospital and the two others died shortly after being admitted. Four of the victims were buried in Kempston parish church, with over 2,000 mourners attending the funerals on 7 August, 1926.

Below: The Luton Borough Mounted Police section was formed in 1909 and here we see them in 1921 awaiting inspection. There were already two ex-cavalrymen serving in the force, and two further local men who were serving in the Lifeguards were appointed as probationary Third Class Constables. For initial training, horses were hired from the local fire brigade and then from the George Hotel. With the onset of the First World War, many officers were called up and the section dwindled away but was re-established when the war finished. Horses were still hired for use, normally from Powdrills stables. The mounted section was often on display for ceremonial duties and also for crowd control, especially during the Peace parade and subsequent riot in 1919. Use of the Mounted section seems to have ceased with the appointment of Mr George Scott as Chief Constable in 1936, and mounted officers were not seen in Luton again until the 1980s when City of London officers assisted in policing Luton Town football matches.

Top right: Bedfordshire Constabulary didn't obtain its first motor car until 1913 when the Chief Constable, Colonel Stevens, purchased a four-seater Arrol Johnson complete with hood, screen, head lamps, horn, spare wheels and tools for £290. It was hoped the car would do the work formerly done by two horses and this proved to be the case as the car travelled 7,164 miles during its first year of service. Bedforshire Police have covered Luton for many years and this picture shows PC 13 Ernest Sibley with a 'Black Maria' vehicle outside Horne Lane station in Bedford sometime in the 1930s. 'Black Maria' was the nickname for secure police vans with separate locked cubicles, used for the transportation of prisoners. One suggested origin of the nickname is that it came from the United States and refers to Maria Lee, a large and fearsome black keeper of a sailors' boarding house who the police would call on for help with difficult prisoners.

Bottom right: Women played no official part in the policing of Bedfordshire until World War Two, when the Women's Auxiliary Police Corps were formed. This supplemented the War Reserve officers (which consisted of ex-policemen) and the Special Constabulary. Although the numbers were small, they made sufficient impression for the Chief Constable to propose that seven regular policewomen be appointed to the county force in 1946. Luton Borough also appointed four female officers in the

same year and here we see WPC's M Leggett and M Arnott in 1947. Initially, recruitment was quite difficult, so a leaflet was published outlining the new role and distributed to local women's service demobilisation centres. The leaflet pointed out the differences between serving in the armed forces and the police: "The police service is a uniformed civilian body and a policewoman can resign if she wishes. She has fixed hours of duty after which she can, in civilian clothes, take part in the amenities enjoyed by the ordinary citizen, and she would probably reside in lodgings with homely people instead of in quarters with a large number of other women. Women constables have the same powers as men and wear a uniform which has greatly improved in style to the point of now being one

of the smartest worn by women today." The pre-entry qualifications were that candidates must be at least 5ft 4ins in height, unmarried or widowed and between 22 and 35 years of age. Over the years, the number of policewomen and the role they play has grown, with female officers in every section of the police force.

Below: As traffic grew rapidly, Britains roads could no longer cope and travel across the country needed much better routes. On 2 November, 1959, the M1 through Bedfordshire was opened. The motorway meant a change for the police and how they covered the roads network and a number of specialist vehicles were purchased to be used solely for patrolling the motorway (or the "Yorkshire Highway" as the road was originally known). Three Ford Zephyr estate cars were bought and converted for police use. Until 1959, police cars had been painted black, but these new vehicles were brilliant white, had a blue flashing beacon on the roof, the word "Police" in large, reflective lettering on the bonnet and a distinctive twotone air horn. There was also a "stop" sign fitted to the rear and a powerful hailing system. By May 1960, Chief Constable, Henry Pratt reported: "Since the opening of the M1, the nineteen mile stretch of motorway in Bedfordshire has been patrolled twenty-four hours a day. It has been found necessary to have two of the motorway patrol vehicles on the road between 8 am and midnight, and all three cars have travelled between 31,000 and 34,000 miles. The crews have dealt with an average of 700 calls a month. The emergency telephones on the motorway, which are linked to Ampthill police station, have produced on average 550 calls a month. In view of the high mileage performed by our three cars, I have arranged for two of our motorcycles to be transferred to the motorway unit in the near future." As Britain's motorway system grew further, the method of policing developed by Bedfordshire Police and surrounding forces for policing the M1 was later adopted throughout the country.

Below: The new "command and control " system at Police HQ, was one of the most significant changes for Bedfordshire Police during the late 70's. This was the construction of a purpose built headquarters at Kempston, Bedford. It enabled a number of departments to be re-located to the new premises when it opened on 17 October, 1978. One of the major benefits of the new building was the implementation of modern technology. The Police National Computer (PNC) had been available to forces for a number of years, but the new facilities meant that this service could be easily accessed by more officers. As a result of the success of the PNC and the proposed move to new premises, it was decided to purchase a computer based "command and control" system to be based at Kempston HQ. The new system would list the location and availability of every officer and vehicle throughout the county. Improved communication systems would also allow operators to contact any officers on duty. All emergency calls would be routed to the control room where operators would direct officers to the incident, with each incident and resultant action being logged onto the system. Three companies tendered to supply the system; Ferranti, Honeywell and Plessey. Honeywell were successful and at a cost of £148,550 the system was purchased and installed at the new HQ. It seems a relatively small sum for such a major change compared to those quoted these days. The control room was still based at "The Pines" (the old HQ in Bedford) until 1979 when the new system became operational. The force was one of just seven forces to employ such a system at this time.

Above: The new town centre Police Station prior to opening. The main stations within Bedford were located at Halsey Rd, Kempston and "The Pines" HQ in Goldington Rd. These were supplemented by a number of smaller sub-stations dotted around the town. The decision was taken to build a large, central, divisional headquarters and construction work began in June 1962 with the station opening in September 1964. In the first annual report of Bedfordshire Constabulary, Chief Constable, Henry Pratt commented "This magnificent Building replaced a very old and inadequate station and provides much improved working conditions and first class facilities for recreation and sport in the gymnasium, the rifle range and the club premises." Although many of the recreational facilities have now gone and the traffic is somewhat busier, Greyfriars is still the main station for the north of Bedfordshire.

WHEN WE WERE KIDS

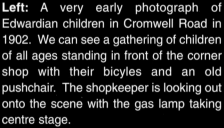

Left: A very early photograph of Edwardian children in Cromwell Road in 1902. We can see a gathering of children of all ages standing in front of the corner shop with their bicyles and an old pushchair. The shopkeeper is looking out onto the scene with the gas lamp taking centre stage.

Above: This is a lovely scene of children in 1906 in Wardown Park, Luton, making daisy chains by the side of the path. The young lad is helping the girls out by picking the daisies whilst they sit on the grass carefully pressing a small thumb nail through the stem of the flower and then threading through the next stem of the chain. They have their warm clothes and hats on so this may be an early spring day in the sunshine. The chap with the cane walking towards them will no doubt give them encouragement to try for a necklace length rather than a short bracelet!

Right: Long trailing skirts were still the order of dress for the young ladies of Luton. Here we see a mother and her possibly teenage daughter in a tree lined corridor in Wardown Park. They both have large rimmed bonnets and could well be out for a Sunday stroll.

Above: The smiling young lad at the front with the net may well have just caught a fish or more likely tiddlers to put in his jam jar. The water is not as deep as it may at first seem, with most of these lads just up to their knees in the middle. It may be a group from two families as they have brought the little ones along with them with mum's and dads reminding them not to get their clothes wet and to stay clear of the deep water. They are certainly not being too boisterous as the two swans just behind them would have flown off some time ago.

Right: More onlookers than bathers here in Wardown Park, but it may well have been a pretty cold day in this scene from 1906

Below: The bobby at the centre of the picture has tucked his white gloves, used when directing traffic, into his uniform to help these seven youngsters across the road from Dunstable Road School in 1934. When Luton became an integrated borough in 1876, it was decided that the town should have its own dedicated police force and Luton Borough Police were formed. This lasted until 1947, when it was absorbed by Bedfordshire Constabulary. If you look closely, you will notice that the officer is wearing a straw helmet. This is made of black and white straw plait, with a leather chin strap and a white metal badge showing the Luton Borough crest. This was unique to Luton Borough officers and used in the warmer weather for greater comfort. Luton was famous for the production of hats, particularly straw boaters. The school is still there, but is now called Beech Hill Community Primary School

Above: Another means of helping the children cross the busy Dunstable Road from the school was introduce in 1938. A crossing attendant ensured the children were helped safely across the road, although with his square sign he would not become known as a 'lollipop man' for some years to come. The streets may have looked quiet in this scene but between the two world wars a staggering 120,000 people were killed in traffic accidents in Britain with the massive increase in vehicles on the roads. This prompted the Minister for Transport at the time, Leslie Hore Belisha, to introduce pedestrian crossings, a 30mph speed limit and, of course, the Belisha Beacons we still recognise today.

The wars years had a major impact not just on fathers and mothers but on children as well. Many were evacuated from London to what was considered a safer place to avoid the heavy bombing which London endured. These children left their homes and families and had no idea where they would be sleeping that night. We can see them clutching their gas masks, cases of packed food and teddy bears and dolls, as they descended on Luton in their thousands. The youngsters were hungry and thirsty when they arrived and Luton people did their best to reassure them and make them feel more comfortable.

Below: School Sports day at Moorlands school in the early 1950s shows team action at its best. Mixed teams racing against each other to get the ball through the 'tunnel' of legs and then the back person runs to the front. Other more athletic events would be taking place and would include: the relay race, the hundred yards dash, the high jump and the long jump. This mixture of boys and girls was only a recent change for the school as it had been a girls only school from its foundation in the 1890s until going co-educational in early1950. No doubt the girls were getting accustomed to the rougher ways of the boys.

Above and top right: In happier times, the energy of Luton children was boundless. Not least for those from the Moorlands School, who we can see here at their sports day in Wardown Park in 1959. A fancy dress race in which the runners are dressed as cowboys, nurses, city gent and Red Riding Hood must have been great fun with everyone laughing, apart from, that is, the cowboy in the lead who is determined to win whatever prize is on offer.

Right: Here we have slightly older children, but only just, as these teenagers at the University of Luton enjoy their Rag Week in 1964. Clearly banjo playing is one of the skills required in this rag week carnival. It was all for a good cause though, as it was in aid of the Freedom from Hunger campaign instigated by the United Nations to raise the global awareness of poverty around the world at the time.

ON THE MOVE

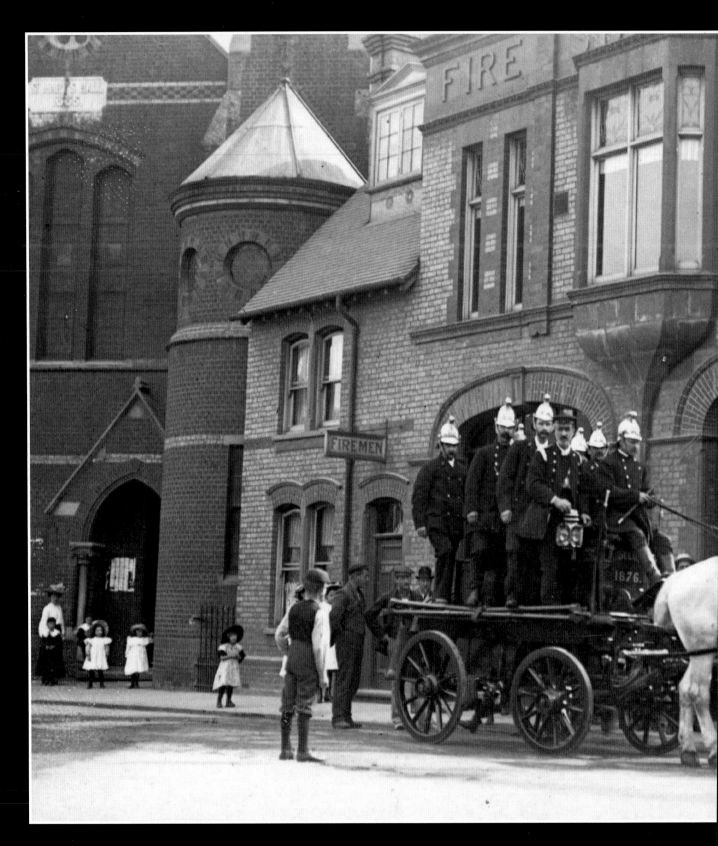

Out with old and in with new. Here are two pictures of the old Fire Station next to St Mary's hall. The two pictures were taken almost 20 years apart. The first with its horse-drawn fire appliance was taken in 1901; the second featuring three 'modern' fire engines was taken in 1931. The early horse-drawn fire engines must have been quite a sight to see racing through the streets on their way to an emergency; the 'fire-engine' itself was in fact a steam-powered water pump so smoke, steam and flames would have been pouring from the engine as it raced to a 'shout'. The firemen had to be stokers and engineers as well as rescue experts. These days firemen are fire officers: back then, and until comparatively recent times, there were no 'fire-women', it being thought that the danger and physical strength need to do the job precluded the fairer sex from undertaking such hazardous and demanding tasks.

Above: That's some building to house a laundry company! These days such an undertaking is more likely to be found operating from an anonymous shed on an even more anonymous industrial estate. Nor would one be collecting and delivering by horse, now it's that ubiquitous 'white van man' rather than a man with a white horse who does that sort of job. But things were different back in 1908 when this photograph was taken.

Meanwhile, our resident expert tells us that what we call a 'carriage' is in fact a 'Tilbury'. Available with or without a hood, the two-wheeled vehicle was developed in the early 19th century by the London firm of Tilbury, coachbuilders based in Mount Street, London. Fast, light, sporty and dangerous, a Tilbury was the ideal vehicle with which to impress young Luton ladies – or so it was said.

Bottom left: Yes, those really are sheep grazing contentedly by the roadside at Round Green. We wonder when was the last time that sight was seen? With references to the area dating back to 1170, Round Green is one of the oldest parts of Luton, The area, however, only became formally within into the boundary of Luton in 1933. In 1908, about the time this photograph was taken, the Luton Tram Service began, with route one starting out in Park Street and terminating at Round Green. The tram service ended in 1931 to be replaced by a buses. There was a large horse chestnut tree next to the modern roundabout outside the Jolly Topers pub. The tree had been a local feature for over 150 years. In 2001, however, after unusually heavy winds, some of the tree's branches blew down and it was deemed hazardous to allow the tree to remain. Happily there have been recent moves to replace it.

Below: The mock Tudor style of the old General Post Office in Cheapside is of of shot. Above the ground floor the stonework gave way to the classic black and white of the Tudor revival so popular in the late 19th and early 20th centuries. Much of Cheapside was of a similar style – now gone. The Royal Mail, later the General Post Office or GPO, was the centre of the national communications network. Not only letters and parcels but also but telegrams and telephone lines all went via the Post Office. Capture these communications hubs and the enemy was crippled. Letters were delivered at least twice a day; postmen dressed in uniforms even used to deliver on Christmas Day. Telegrams would be delivered immediately by boys on bicycles. Today, with e-mails and texting, such a high standard of service is no longer needed.

Above: Christ Church and Upper George Street was captured by the cameraman in 1929. All's well with the world, or at least everyone thought it was. The war was ten years in the past, and a post-war boom had increased standards of living. The decade would be known as the 'Roaring Twenties' and was remembered for dances such as the Charleston and the Black Bottom, as well as for introducing cinema to a worldwide audience. Stars such as Charlie Chaplin, Mary Pickford and Douglas Fairbanks became international celebrities and millionaires. Alas, any complacency was ill-founded. The Wall Street Crash was only days away when this photo was taken, and a decade of economic misery lay just around the corner. Meanwhile particularly worthy of note is the milk churn and hand cart on the right. Before door step deliveries of milk in milk bottles was introduced, milk was sold direct from the churn, and dispensed into housewives' own jugs.

Bottom left: The first definite tramway scheme was placed before a joint meeting of the town council's highways and electric lighting committees in May 1900. It was not, however, until October 1901 that the council appointed a tramways committee with ex-Alderman Giddings as chairman. The committee entered into negotiations with J.G. White and Co Ltd with a view to obtaining from it an offer to construct, equip and lease tramways in Luton. White and Co submitted ta proposal for a period of five or 15 years, at the option of the council, the capital to be provided by the Corporation, and a rent, equal to interest and sinking fund charges during the term of the lease, to be paid by White and Co. The system's twelve two-decker tramcars each provided seating for 54 passengers - 22 inside and 32 outside. A 'car-shed' to house them was erected in Park Street on a plot of land adjoining the East Ward Recreation Ground.

Below: Tram Number 4 is caught here in Dunstable Road. The Luton Corporation's initial fleet which began service in 1908 consisted of 12 (Nos. 1-12) United Electric Car open-top double-deckers. They would be the only new tramcars ever purchased for the system. The trams operated from the outset in a green and white livery, with Luton Corporation Tramways displayed on the lower body panels. Working as a tram driver was a rotten job, being out in the open all day in the cold wet. No one at the time seems to have thought to enclose the cab – after all drivers of horse-drawn vehicles were always out in the fresh air. With the coming of the trams the character of Dunstable Road changed, existing houses were turned into shops and their front gardens paved over. Further out from Luton new buildings sprang up as 'commuting' became easier.

The Pickford business can be traced back to the 17th century when the Pickford family began a small carrier business in Manchester. The name Pickfords is still synonymous with moving house.

Here, in 1920, is Pickfords' Luton furniture storage facility together with a fine three-horse pantechnicon pictured in the days before motor lorries and diesel power replaced our equine friends. Rather a lot of horses were still employed by

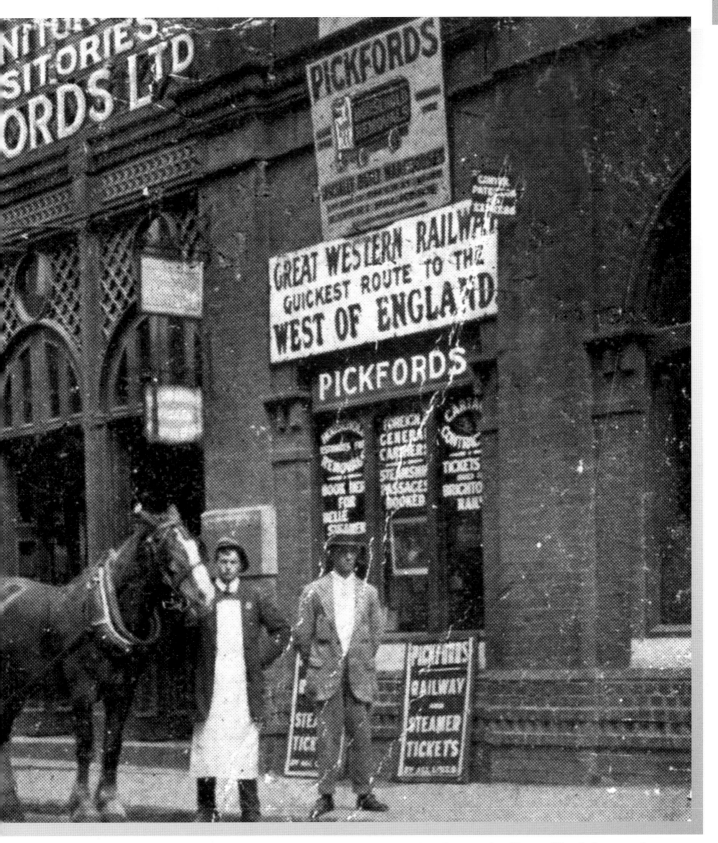

Pickfords back then: in 1919, the firm owned 1,580 horses and 1,900 horse vehicles. Their nemesis was represented by just 46 motor vehicles. Members of the original Pickford family sold the firm in the 19th century; in 1919 it was sold again, this time to the Hayes Wharf Cartage Company Limited .Since then the firm has passed through several owners, and is now part of Moving Services Group UK Ltd.

Above: 'Drinka a Pinta Milka Day' says the advert from the Milk Marketing Board on the hoarding in the background of this scene. The slogan was first introduced to the British public in 1958, and continued in use for several years, well into the 1960s. Despite the horse and cart this photo appears to be from the 1960s rather than the 1950s. Drinka Pinta Milk a Day became something of a national catchphrase and was soon on everyone's slips. Comedian Tony Hancock even called one episode of his famous television comedy series Drinka Pinta Milka a Day! This picture, and talk of one comedy classic, soon leads to another: Steptoe and Son, the dysfunctional father and son team of rag and bone men who, together with their horse Hercules, lived at Oil Drum Lane, Shepherds Bush. These days rag and bone men seem to have all become recycling specialists. Meanwhile, does anyone know what that strange cry they shouted out made actually meant?

Top right: There are a few interesting points within this photograph taken at Shaw and Kilburn's Vauxhall Garage, in Dunstable Road, in the early 1940s. The first obvious one is that two of the attendants are women, both in white overalls. The importance of personal service was very high on the list for these petrol stations hoping to attract custom from the growing number of cars on the roads. The second point is the variety of petrol brands on offer including Esso, Shell, National and Cleveland Discol, all quite different to the branded petrol stations of today.

Right: A group of day-trippers in the 1940s possibly off to London to see the sights, or maybe even to the coast. What is clear is with the smiles and 'Sunday best' they are all looking forward to a lovely day out and the journey on the 'coach' behind them will be a big part of the trip.

Luton railway station is pictured here in 1976. In some ways not much has changed. The trains and carriages look very similar to those of today. Just a decade earlier the last of the steam trains were still thundering down the line. Diesel, then electric, trains replaced steam in the 1960s, much to the dismay of train spotters who once infested stations, bridges and viaducts in vast numbers. The various railway companies had been nationalised just after the war, becoming first British Railways, and then simply 'BR'. When this photo was taken BR had yet to be broken up and sold off to today's Railtrack and the various companies which now run on the rail network. Perhaps the biggest change on the railways since 1976, however, has been the progressive removal of smoking carriages. Back then non-smoking passengers were often annoyed by cigarette and pipe-smokers in neighbouring seats – today they are annoyed by a new menace, the mobile phone addict.

Right: Transport in Luton took on all shapes and sizes and this auto truck was no exception. It was based at the Electrolux factory in Oakley Road, a major employer in the town. The truck, we assume, was to transport goods around the large factory, but here we see Miss Electrolux, Mary Taylor, chatting with workers at the site. Electrolux produced vacuum cleaners and refrigerators in the early days and became one of Europe's largest refrigerator manufacturers before the factory closed in 1998.

Left: Number 31 to the airport anyone? By 1969, a fifth of all holiday flights from the UK departed from Luton Airport. Or maybe the passengers are actually about to get off the single-decker at the next stop and do some shopping? Just passing Barratts and Burtons on its way to Luton airport bus fleet number 102 is pictured here in 1967.

Above: 'Hold tight please'. The Bristol Lodekka was a low-height double-decker bus built by Bristol Commercial Vehicles. It was the first production bus design to have no step up from the passenger entrance throughout the lower deck. Bristol manufactured over 5,200 Lodekkas from 1949 to 1968, as a standard double-deck vehicle. With all examples bodied by Eastern Coach Works in Lowestoft, they had a traditional half-cab design and a lower floor level allowing a low overall height. The earlier LD-series and the later FL and FS had a rear platform, but the FSF and FLF had a front entrance. Most were powered by 5 or 6-cylinder Gardner engines, with fewer having a Bristol or Leyland power unit. With the arrival of more modern 'OMO' or one man operated buses, such as the Leyland Atlantean and Bristol VRT (the Lodekka's successor), many Lodekkas found themselves relegated to driver training duties.

Above: Tom Sheaf started the Luton-based Sheaf's Dairies with his wife in 1936 in Wellington Road. The iconic milk floats were an ever-present sight on the streets of Luton for many years, with the rounds men and women arriving at 4am to stock up with milk, eggs and cream. As the business grew and tastes changed the company moved to Latimer Road in the late 1970s and added yoghurt, mineral water and flavoured milks to their products. The milk men and women were an important social part of Luton life as they inconspicuously kept an eye on the households and older people on their rounds. Here we see the floats parked up in the Latimer Road depot.

Bottom left and below: The Luton Girls Choir found they needed to travel far and wide as their reputation grew over the years. They sang infront of every member of the British royal family between 1936 and 1976 and can be seen (left) arriving for a Royal Command Performance. Their average age was 18 and to ensure it remained a 'girls' choir, 23 was the upper age limit, or marriage would also exclude them from singing. They raised thousands of pounds over the years for charity and sang for free themselves, just enjoying being in the choir and travelling with friends.

In the second photograph (below) they can be seen boarding a KLM Lockheed Constellation aeroplane bound for Australia and New Zealand in 1959. The girls travelled 35,000 miles and gave 93 concerts on their three month tour and were rapturously received wherever they performed. The choir disbanded in 1976 but a reunion was held in 1986 to celebrate the 50th anniversary of its formation. The difference between the fashion and clothing can be clearly seen between the two photographs, but the one thing that remains constant, is the happy smiling faces of every girl in the choir.

I t's a long time ago, but Luton was opened on 16 July, 1938, and was considered the northern terminal for London. During the war it was used for military aircraft but civil use started again in 1952. It was the next ten years that saw a real growth in passengers through

the introduction of the 'package holiday'. By 1972, Luton had become Britain's most profitable airport. There was some decline with tour operators going bust, but with new investments and new management, the airport again thrived becoming the UK's fifth largest airport today with over 9 million passengers a year. The inside of the old terminal can be seen above with a somewhat 'staged' photograph showing the facilities on offer around the time the M! completion saw more passengers travelling from Luton. Just beyond the Humber and Ford Prefect cars we can see a Lockheed L149 Constellation propeller driven plane which was scrapped not long after this photograph was taken in 1965. Another plane at the airport in Sept 1966 was civilianised Douglas Invader WW-II bomber belonging to the London Company, Geophysics Ltd being used as a spotter plane possibly to map in detail the local topography and take high specification aerial photographs.

THE WAY WE WERE!

Each generation thinks of itself as modern at every stage of life and yet we are all relics and mementoes of our own history. As time goes by, we try to hang on to our more modish and fashionable behaviour and attitudes, sometimes with the thought that we can defy the passing of time with our constant recreation of 'the past'. Even so, most people enjoy looking back and remembering with affection things done or achieved and comparing the context of their early lives with improvements sometimes made in more recent times. Things often seem not to be as good as in the 'olden days', but most of the time we are not looking at a level playing field. Inevitably, many of our childhood memories, whatever our age now, are of endless summers and snow-filled winters, a sort of historically appropriate version of Dylan Thomas's 'A Child's Christmas in Wales'. But, for all of us, time marches on and, as we get older, it seems strange that we find ourselves attempting to explain to a nine year old god-daughter that there was life of a sort before computers, emphasising simultaneously our incredibly ancient origins!

Wartime experiences and memories often define generations, although with involvement in more recent conflicts, even this timeline has had to be redefined. The progress in radio and TV development has outstripped most people's imagination and provided a sometimes obsessive and questionable way of filling our days. Until the middle of the 20th century, children often had to use their own imagination, inventiveness and creativity. The streets were filled with groups of children of different ages pretending to be somebody, somewhere and something else. This was fun for most, freeing and gentle in its stimulation, and engendered a relevant and satisfactory competitiveness conducive to learning.

This page: Outdoors including in the playground, improvisation was the name of the game. You didn't need a ball for football - a tightly bound bundle of rags or clothes would do. There were games that matched the seasons, conkers for example. Those determined to win used foul and dishonest ways to convert the simple conker into a hard and

Below centre: In the 1930s, toys were still quite simple, for boys and girls. In a society that continued to place the emphasis on women as home makers and child producers, toymakers were still making a lot of money from selling pretty little dolls to pretty little girls, banking on their softness for small, defenceless creatures in their own image. This wonderful picture, taken in 1950, shows two such little girls enjoying posing for a 'family' photograph, repeated no doubt twenty years later as the real thing. Note the grittily determined, no-nonsense expression of the young lady at the back and the rather shyer, slightly myopic expression of the seated young lady with hair that, possibly, she has spent the rest of her life not being able to 'do a thing with'!

Below: The influence of Errol Flynn in the 1940s is obvious here in a game involving bows and arrows. His playing of Robin Hood against Olivia de Havilland as Maid Marian had a ground-breaking impact for some little boys that remained with them to their teenage years (and in some cases even longer!). Cinema has always had an influence on children's re-enactment and performance of stories and fables. Certainly children in the 1940s rarely complained about boredom or having nothing to do. They simply grasped the nettle and worked out what they could turn it into and did it together.

unyielding boulder to cheat their way to success. Later in the year it was marbles with those wonderful glass beads put to aggressive and destructive use to determine who was top dog. There were also collecting activities, usually involving cards with familiar faces, often of footballers or film stars. Playground games were often determined by gender, with the differences usually marked by the polarising of physical prowess and single-mindedness on the one hand and a softer camaraderie and togetherness on the other. All the equipment and artefacts used in play were simple, often loud and often extremely irritating in their use and application, but great fun!

Above: Many Bethel Chapels followed the mission statement, 'to turn the lost into the found and the faithless into the faithful'. The word 'Bethel' is taken from two Hebrew words, 'bêt' and 'el', meaning the house of God. 'Chapel' is derived from the Latin 'cappella', meaning cloak. The building, therefore, provided a secret place where dissenters could worship God. Chapels were originally breakaway places, shattering the mould by providing a place of worship for those who objected to the status quo. In the dark days of the 1920s, poverty was rife. Many poor families had little in the way of either hope or sustenance. They simply got poorer.

Right: The group of unknown kiddies, pictured here in the late 19th century, were the lucky ones. Dressed up in their finery, including the borrowing of a few fathers' flat caps, they looked the picture of health. In all probability, they would live to a ripe old age. Some of their siblings were not so fortunate. Insanitary living conditions for the working classes, poor diets and no such things as antibiotics, penicillin or mass immunisation meant that youngsters fell prey to a host of childhood diseases, scarlet fever, whooping cough and measles, to name but three.

relied on outside toilets and the tin bath in the yard that was brought inside on a Saturday night, whether you needed an all over scrub or not. Waiting in front of a roaring fire, with kettles of boiling water being prepared, was part of the routine. This little lass obviously had her own individual model. Young Doreen or Dorothy, whatever her name was, could make the fun of bathtime last right up to the final 'Come on young lady, beddie-byes' was repeated in an exasperated voice.

Above: Little pedal cars were all the rage, especially for young boys, in the 1930s. Motoring was booming and toy manufacturers spotted the opportunity of a new niche in the market. While less affluent parents bought their children scooters for Christmas, Santa Claus packed his sleigh with imitations of real motorcars for the offspring of the wealthy. Some cars actually featured windows that really moved, working horns and lights, real chrome, bonnet ornaments, white wall tyres and custom paint. Many of the cars were made from metal, though this became less likely in the 1940s as the war effort demanded that such materials were channelled into the manufacture of military ordnance.

Right: Even in the middle of the last century, not all homes had bathrooms. Some of the older properties

Below: Conditions may have been grim on occasions but there was usually time for a warm smile and friendly chat in the street. These were the days when people routinely left their doors unlocked or open, without fear of someone running off with their television. Of course, they didn't have a television, but you know what we mean! These days the neighbourly culture which we used to take for granted has disappeared from many areas and some people seem to know the characters in the popular soap operas better than the people next door. It would be unusual, to say the least, to see a modern housewife scrubbing the pavement outside her house in this day and age.

appliances or white goods to make the task of running the house any easier. Many families lived in terraced housing, some of it back to back, with outdoor lavvies, where you learned to whistle

with one foot against the door in case someone else attempted to enter this little smelly enclave of privacy. Many houses still had a tin bath that was dragged in from the yard and filled with kettle after kettle of boiling water before family members took it in turn to soak themselves. These photographs show typical scenes from life at the time; families and communities were close knit, sharing each other's joys and sorrows. It was quite common to lend a neighbour a helping hand in times of need and this was often more than just a cup of sugar. Friendships were formed that lasted a lifetime.

Top right and right: At one time, Monday was the traditional washday for many. For working class families, the burden fell upon mum. Her role as a housewife meant that the day was spent boiling clothes in a tub and wringing them out through the mangle before pegging out on the line in a back yard, or similar. Before the days of sophisticated washing powders and rubber gloves, reddened hands were her reward and yet there were still beds to be made, carpets to beat and lino to wash. The children needed feeding and the evening meal had to be ready when dad got home. It was hard work and there were few, if any, modern electrical

Above: When the baby boomer generation went to school in the early 1950s, it had benefited from the 1944 Education Act that brought free education to all primary and secondary-aged children. For the first time, there was a level playing field, to use a school based analogy. Of course, that field had its bumps and muddy portions because perfection and complete equality could not be guaranteed. Those going to school in leafy suburbs tended to do better than those where slag heaps overlooked the grimy villages. But, at least working class kids had the chance of better and further education. Such lofty thoughts were not in the minds of these youngsters enjoying the activities in this Primary School playground. The lad in the background obviously fancied himself as Roy Rogers or Tom Mix as he played on the rocking horse and checked behind him that pesky injuns were not on his trail. The girls, of course, enjoyed dressing the dolls as another couple had fun on the see-saw. They did not bump it too hard as the lads did when they had their turn.

Below: A typical scene from what looks like a mid-1950s classroom. From the look of them, it would seem that they were part of the Junior School. This however, was a fee paying establishment, one of many that gave those families with money to spare a flying start when it came to their children's education. No-one spoke of equality under the 1944 Act here. It was a daily routine of cramming for the 11 plus as passing that was the be all and end all. Art, music, drama and science could wait. It was inky fingers, dip pens, sitting still and following rules. Education was not to be enjoyed but endured. The best days of your life? Pass.

Above: Out of necessity, road safety has become a major issue for all of us in our lifetimes and has been written into the school curriculum since the middle of the 20th century. As we can see in photographs from earlier in the last century that appear in this book, children played games in the streets and rode their bicycles on the carriageway with little danger to life or limb. With the steadily increasing traffic in the 1930s, safety became an obvious and challenging issue and, with accident statistics rising alarmingly, the government of the day was obliged to take action. Driving tests were introduced, Belisha Beacon crossings appeared in towns and cities and that well-known bestseller, The Highway Code, was formulated and published. In this photograph taken in 1950, youngsters are given instruction on a model roadway system. Stop, look and listen were watchwords drummed into children together with instruction on how to signal correctly and how to use crossings safely. In later years, we saw the Tufty Club, the Green Cross Code and, frighteningly, a fully permed Kevin Keegan advising us on why it was NOT a good idea to run out from behind parked cars! Sometimes, it all seemed a little light-hearted, but at least it got the point over.

Right: When Ernest Evans asked whether it was a bird or a plane up there and answered himself by telling us that it was a twister, a craze was born that swept dance floors across the western world. He also made sure that countless numbers of children would be embarrassed at weddings, 21st dos and parties during the 1990s as their parents risked hernias and heart attacks attempting to twist the night away whilst their offspring raised their eyes to heaven. Evans was a fan of the 1950s rocker Fats Domino and used his name as the inspiration for becoming known as Chubby Checker. Oddly, his first big hit in Britain was in 1963 with 'Let's Twist Again', a follow up to 'The Twist', a record that only became very popular the following year. By 1963, when this couple attempted to keep their seams straight as they gyrated in the front room to the music from their Dansette record player,

WORKING LIFE

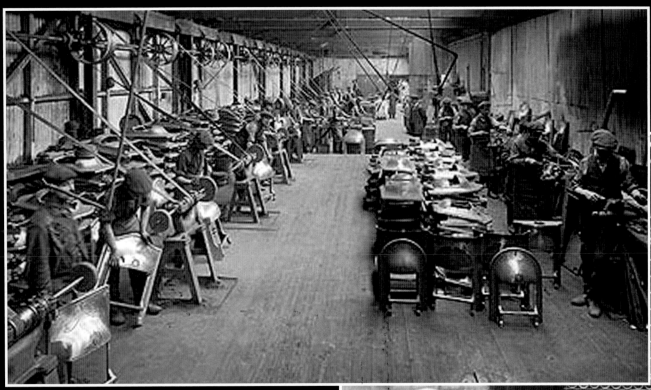

Above: The interior of the grinding shop at the Diamond Foundry, part of the Luton factory of the Davis Gas Stove Company Limited, was captured by the cameraman in June 1913. The main components of not only gas stoves but also of fire surrounds and other cast iron articles were made in the foundry, then brought here to be polished or have imperfections removed through grinding and filing. What is particularly interesting here is the very clear view of the belt driven mechanisms common to most factories of the period. Today individual machines are powered by their own electric motors: in the past factories would typically be powered by a single coal-fired steam engine. Power from the engine would turn a long shaft down the length of a factory and individual machine would in turn take power off by attaching belts to wheels on the turning shaft. Grinding was a dangerous and dirty job: it was said that you weren't a real grinder if you still had ten fingers.

Below: Number 41 High Town Road was a hardware dealer's in the late 19th and early 20th centuries. For forty years or so in the mid-20th century it was a branch of Home and Colonial Stores Limited, a grocery business. In the 21st century it became a Polish delicatessen serving the large local Eastern European population. Home & Colonial Stores was once one of the United Kingdom's largest retail chains. Its formation of a vast chain of retail stores in the late 1920s was the first step in the development of a UK food retail market dominated by a small number of large companies. The firm was founded by Julius Drewe who in 1883 went into partnership with John Musker selling groceries at a small shop in Edgware Road in London. They subsequently opened stores in Islington, Birmingham and Leeds. The shops mainly sold tea and by 1885 they were trading as the Home & Colonial Tea Association. Between 1924 and 1931, several stores, including Liptons merged with Home & Colonial to form a company with over 3,000 branches.

Above: What are these workmen up to in George Street? They are obviously installing something in the roadbed but exactly what is unclear. In fact it is traffic lights. Before lights were introduced the job of controlling traffic fell to the police. Though today it is rare to see a policeman directing traffic it was commonplace well into the 1960s. Although Britain's first traffic lights were installed in 1868, outside the Houses of Parliament, in London, it was many more years before they arrived in Bedfordshire. In Luton it was a major event when these lights were erected at the corner of George Street and Chapel Street in October 1949. People came from miles around just to look at the new-fangled traffic management devices. The George Street lights were eventually removed when the road was pedestrianised.

Bottom left and right: Vauxhall's sheet metal finishing department was a hive of activity when this photograph was taken. Indeed there hardly seems room to work. The company was founded in Vauxhall, London, in 1857 by Scottish engineer Alexander Wilson. Wilson and Company became the Vauxhall Iron Works in 1897. Vauxhall built its first car, a five-horsepower model steered using a tiller, with two forward gears and no reverse gear, in 1903. This led to a better design which was made available for sale. The company moved the majority of its production to Luton in 1905 where in 1907 the company adopted its modern name of Vauxhall Motors. During World War II, car production at Luton was suspended to allow Vauxhall to work on the new Churchill tank, taking it from specification to production in less than a year, and assembled there (as well as at other sites). Over 5,600 Churchill tanks were built. Luton also produced around 250,000 lorries for the war effort. In the 1960s, Vauxhall acquired a reputation for making rust-prone models, though in truth most other car manufacturers were just as bad. The corrosion protection built into models was tightened up significantly, but the reputation dogged the company until the early 1980s.

Below: Until 1925 General Motors assembled in Brazil the trucks manufactured at its Canadian works. Such trucks were marketed as 'British Chevrolet'. After GM took ownership of Vauxhall Motors, production was transferred from Hendon to Luton, Vauxhall's headquarters, production commencing there in 1929. The AC and LQ models were produced at Luton from 1929 to 1931, and styled as the 'Chevrolet Bedford'. The AC was bodied as a light van (12 cwt), and the LQ in a wide variety of roles, including a lorry, ambulance, van and bus versions. The name 'Chevrolet' was dropped, and the first 'Bedford' was produced in April 1931. By the time this photograph was taken of the Bedford truck assembly line in Luton over 250 trucks and vans were being produced every working day for export to over 130 different countries.

"The 'No Hat' Craze Will Mean No Hat Trade For Us. We Ask Our Employees To Set A Good Example". It's rather ironic that the four young ladies in the far right photo from 1940 are not in fact wearing hats! With the outbreak of war in 1939, however, perhaps the government had a part to play in the 'No hat Craze' – money not spent on luxuries could be spent on guns, planes and ships instead. Whatever the

GRAY & HORN.
ENGLISH PLAIT MERCHANTS.
LUTON.

Connor Hat FACTORY

SKETCHLEY DRY CLEANING

the 'No hat craze' has lasted for over seventy years. The catchy advertising slogan of the 1960s, 'Get ahead, get a hat', coined by the British Hat Council in 1965, did little to turn the tide. Luton's hat industry had been famous not just in Britain but throughout the world. Its hat factories such as Connor's did not simply sustain their own workers but those of subsidiary industries such as cotton merchants and straw plait merchants like Gray & Horn as well as dyers and milliners. Even in 1940, however, the local trade which had its origins in the early 19th century, had long been in decline. Hat making had reached its peak in Luton in the 1870s. The 1871 census shows that out of a total population of 17,316 living in the township of Luton, 5,615 men women and children were employed in plaiting, hat making and allied trades.

Connolly Homes PLC
New Homes Better Built

Now based at Manor Farm Court, Manor Road, Lower Sundon, the well known firm of Connolly Homes Plc was founded half a century ago by Michael F. Connolly, whose early background in the building industry made it possible for the development of the company to be based on a foundation of practical experience. In the intervening years the name Connolly has become synonymous with quality housebuilding in the region.

The Connolly name has not just been associated with the building trade: through it's founder's philanthropy the business has made a far greater impact on the community than simply providing new homes for our ever-growing population.

When young Michael Connolly arrived in Luton from his native Aughamore, in Co. Mayo, Ireland, back in 1958 with only the possessions he carried, little could he have dreamed of the major company he would build, and the national house-building awards he would one day win.

"We got off the train at Kings Cross Station with only what we could carry," he recalled, "but that was the story of our generation."

Michael was trained as a joiner in his native Ireland; however, abandoning earlier plans to be a woodwork teacher, he came to England and started doing small jobs for the then Luton Corporation.

For five years Michael worked hard and saved even harder, impelled by a burning ambition to be his own boss and to have his own building firm. It was the start of a new era, indeed everything was changing; a new Labour Government, Dr Who, the Beatles, and above all a new wave of national optimism as at last the post-war economy picked up speed, and thousands more people felt it might be safe at last to buy their own home.

Michael was able to buy his first, small site - at Harlington - with the help of a friendly bank manager from what was then the Westminster Bank.

"Bank managers were very different in those days." Michael remembered. "He'd get on his bike and actually come to look at a site".

*Above: Founder, Michael Connolly. **Below:** The first Connolly bungalows built in Harlington.*

then, in 1969, to newly built premises in Sarum Road.

The site included an old house, for which the tenant was paying the previous owners, the Co-op, £1 a week. Michael rehoused him in Stockingstone Road, and kept his rent at just £1 a week until he died.

The Sarum Road site – to become known as Connolly House - would not only become the Group's head office but also house a joiners' shop, plant department workshop and storage space.

By the end of the Sixties, half of Connolly's business was private housing and the other half contract work for local authorities.

Three pairs of semi-detached houses were built on the site; they would be the first of many.

Meanwhile, the tiny firm enjoyed none of the luxuries which would be taken for granted in later years; everyone involved had to be prepared to do anything. "In the early days we couldn't even afford to employ anyone to answer the phone," said Michael. Meanwhile, as Michael also recalls, "Back in those days there was no such thing as a show house, and there were very few new houses advertised." But money spent on advertising would pay dividends. The first advertisement worked well, and the company received a stack of replies expressing interest and they soon sold those three pairs of semis.

In the early 1970s, the group started a company in Devon with a further building operation established at Holywood, in County Down, Northern Ireland. By now the Company was building up to 1,000 houses a year between their three operations in Luton, Devon and Northern Ireland.

Next came Abbey Close, a 21-plot site in Ampthill, followed by a third site in nearby Clophill, where more than 70 homes were built.

The business went from strength to strength, fulfilling Michael's 'game plan' which at the time was to double the number of legal completions each year. As a result those early days when the young Michael Connolly would do not just the woodwork, but also the plumbing and electrics too, were long gone!

The thriving firm soon grew out of it's 'office' in the greenhouse at the side of Michael's family home in Ashburnham Road, Luton, moving to proper offices in Cardiff Road and

Above: In the 1960s Ampthill Rural District Council handed over the 2,000th house it had completed since the war. Michael Connolly is centre picture. *Below:* A Connolly home in Greenfield.

By the mid-1970s recession hit and many building firms went under, however, with careful management and not a little hard work and worry, the Connolly Group weathered the storm.

"It was a tough time then and I had an ulcer chopped out to prove it!" commented Michael.

Even in those hard times the firm still managed to start it's own apprenticeship scheme which although eventually discontinued has led to an even more widespread legacy today.

Connolly Homes PLC was now employing a workforce of more than 250 and building around 350 houses a year across the Home Counties and in Northern Ireland; from two-bedroomed homes to exclusive five-bedroomed family houses all offering the latest in contemporary features. Pride in the job was as evident then as it is today.

"Our policy at Connolly Homes PLC is to develop and provide a range of houses in various styles and sizes, which reflect our high standards and good reputation." said Michael. "All our homes demonstrate our attention to detail and dedication to using traditional building methods together with the latest technology, offering a home that is both architecturally and environmentally pleasing."

The company had by now become the largest private house builder in Bedfordshire and had won a string of accolades, including several NHBC Top 100 awards.

Down the decades the company has constructed a multitude of developments ranging from starter homes to detached residences in exclusive locations throughout Bedfordshire, Buckinghamshire, Cambridgeshire and Northamptonshire.

All Connolly Homes developments are carefully and efficiently controlled from the Group headquarters at their new offices in Lower Sundon, near Luton. The company prides itself on it's continued attention to detail and staff training and as a result has won many prestigious awards

Above: The late Eric Morecombe pictured in the 1960s as a guest at the opening of the Langford, Bedfordshire, development. Below inset: 1970s Executive Luton homes built by Connollys. Bottom: A street of Connolly homes in Caddington, Bedfordshire.

over the years including the Daily Express 'Housebuilder of the Year' and many other National House Building Council awards.

In recent years, Connolly Homes were most proud to be awarded the title 'Best Regional House Builder', Beds & Bucks in the Which Home South East Awards and the R.I.B.A. Regional Award for excellence in housing design.

As a housebuilder, Connolly Homes PLC's policy is to provide homes in various styles and sizes that are well built, well designed and well specified; homes that give great value, reflect the firm's high standards and enhance it's good reputation. Connolly houses are built using a combination of traditional building methods coupled with the latest technology to provide a home that is both comfortable to live in and economical to run.

The good works of the Foundation to date include substantial and ongoing grants and donations committed to schools, hospice care and a welfare care centre for the elderly, together with other schemes. A key aspect is the provision of student grants to assist young people with their further and higher education.

In recognition of his philanthropy towards the elderly and to the education for young people in Bedfordshire, Michael Connolly was made an honorary Doctor of Science by the University of Bedfordshire.

This page: Artist impressions of Connolly Homes from townhouses, left, to substantial detached homes above and below.

For half a century the firm has worked with it's suppliers, contractors, local authorities and local communities to become one of the most reputable house builders in the South East. However there is one key difference with the company – it is owned by a Charitable Trust.

This unique situation came about when Michael Connolly's wife Kathleen died unexpectedly; he wanted to set up a charity in her memory which would assist the young and elderly in local communities. Michael gifted his shares in Connolly Homes PLC to a new charity, The Kathleen and Michael Connolly Foundation UK Ltd – the Connolly Foundation.

The Kathleen and Michael Connolly Foundation

Putting Something Back

The Kathleen and Michael Connolly Foundation (UK) Ltd has two main objectives. Firstly, the relief of poverty and deprivation generally, in particular by providing accommodation and assistance for persons who are disadvantaged, and wholly or partly unable to make such provisions for themselves.

The second objective is the provision of education and training facilities, especially funding vocational training and training facilities for young people.

The Foundation provides grants and donations to schools, school students, hospice care and welfare care and receives funding from it's shareholding in Connolly Homes PLC, bestowed on it by the company's founder Michael Connolly.

The Foundation provides funding and grants for a range of projects which include annual grants to school leavers moving into Further Education, supporting capital projects for the elderly and the terminally ill, and supporting multi-purpose projects giving provision for young people, further education and for the retired population.

Investments in the community included matched funding and technical support from Connolly Homes for Stratton Upper School in Biggleswade to rebuild their school farm buildings. This included a covered yard for animal handling and construction practice areas as well as construction of a new building. The school farm provides a unique educational facility with hands on care for a variety of farm animals from pigs and sheep to ducks and chickens. The school also makes profits from sales from the farm which are re-invested in repairs, equipment and running costs.

Elsewhere Keech Hospice Care benefitted when the Foundation made a substantial grant to assist in completion of a new in-patient unit. This was donated through the 'building for better care' appeal and the in-

Top: Founders, Kathleen and Michael Connolly. *Left:* The new IPU Unit for Keech Hospice Care supported by The Connolly Foundation. *Above:* Michael Callanan, Connolly Foundation Trustee (right) donates a cheque to the Stratton School Farm Appeal.

Six schools, Sharnbrook Upper School and Community College, Cardinal Newman Catholic School, Stratton Upper School, St Thomas More Catholic School, Redborne Upper and Biddenham International School, have also received capital grants from the foundation. These helped equip new IT suites, physical activity centres, and 6th Form common rooms.

Each year the Foundation has continued to provide grants for students moving into further and higher education to help them on their way into employment. This has been a growth project for the Foundation which partners the University of Bedfordshire as well. Students have continued to express their gratitude for the support given and it has been wonderful for the Foundation to follow the progress of some of them as they stay in touch via social media through college and into employment.

So, the Foundation turns full circle - from the day Michael Connolly stepped off the train as a young man at King's Cross station with nothing but a suitcase, to building up his own successful company and now – a legacy that helps other young people and the elderly get more from their own lives, just as he did.

patient unit (IPU) provides specialised palliative care whilst at all times aiming to maintain dignity and patient choice.

The Foundation also pledged significant funds to 'kick start' fund raising for a new building project on behalf of Leonard Cheshire Disability which resulted in the redevelopment of the care home. The total cost of the re-build was £515,000 and completely refurbished the entire home providing everyone who uses it with a range of new facilities.

The Bedfordshire Cheshire Home, Agate House, in Ampthill, provides continuous nursing and care services in a one-storey building offering accommodation for thirty-two severely disabled people between the ages of 18 and 65.

A community welfare centre received 50% funding towards the £250,000 cost of a new activity centre after it was left needing a new home when the council re-developed the original site. Technical support was also provided by Connolly Homes and they constructed the building for no profit, at cost only. The Foundation provided professional advice from beginning to end whereupon Michael Connolly handed over the keys to the new 'Kathleen Connolly House', a hub for community activity.

Top left: Michael Connolly opening Kathleen Connolly House in his late wife's memory. **Below:** Opening Day of St Thomas More School Activity Centre in October 2009. Left to right: Martin Cross, Olympic Champion; Michael Callanan, Connolly Foundation Trustee; Alan Lee, St Thomas More Headteacher and Stephen O'Brien, Diocese of Northampton.

Hayward Tyler

Quality, Innovation and Service since 1815

Hayward Tyler, based in Kimpton Road, Luton, has been in business for some 200 years.

Down the millennia, intelligent observation of the behaviour of water in its various states has led to many invaluable discoveries and inventions: Archimedes who noticed that the level of his bathwater rose when he got in, cried, 'Eureka!' and went on to develop the Archimedes principle; the domestic kettle inspired James Watt to invent a new steam engine; and Joseph Bramah, working from similar observations, changed the face of industry by inventing the steam press.

Joseph Bramah also invented continuous carbonation and the water closet. Many of his inventions were turned to practical use by his student William Russell, who in 1815 founded a business in St John's Street in the City of London, manufacturing water closets, hydraulic presses and soda water machines. William Russell died in 1835 and his company was taken over by Hayward Tyler, whose family had begun trading in 1783 as tea urn manufacturers. In 1837, Mr Tyler moved his company to premises in nearby Whitecross Street. Here the manufacture of soda water machines continued and the brass foundry side of the business developed too; screw-down cocks and various brasswork items for use in the plumbing trade were introduced at this time and remained on the company's catalogue for the next hundred years.

In 1855, the company changed hands when Hayward Tyler died and his widow sold the firm to a relative, Robert Luke Howard, for £7,500. Robert Howard was himself an engineer who had served his apprenticeship with Messrs Fowler and Fry, of Bristol.

The young man brought his own ideas to the company; new products added to the list during the next few decades included machinery for making aerated bread, and the Universal Pump, a single-cylinder steam pump with internal valve gear which was introduced in 1869 and superseded the Direct Acting Pump.

Robert's youngest brother, Eliot, had joined the firm in 1863, and to cope with expansion some adjoining cowsheds had been purchased in 1866 and converted into a new workshop, but the business carried on expanding. The decision was taken to buy land outside London, and a good site was found in a little village called Luton, to the north of the city, which in 1872 was just beginning to develop as an industrial centre.

Retaining the London premises as Head Office, the company built a new factory on land near the Great Northern Railway in Luton. With various members of the Howard family investing in the venture, Hayward Tyler became the largest company in Luton at that time; and before the end of the century its workforce was to be instrumental in the formation of the Luton Co-operative Society. The company began to take on Government contracts, building packing presses and in 1878 producing a hay pressing plant for Woolwich Dockyard. That same year the Rider hot air engine was produced, probably at the instigation of one of the firm's American associates, Mr Benson. By that time Robert Samuel Lloyd, a cousin of Robert and Eliot Howard (who was also directly descended from the family which founded Lloyd's Bank), had also joined the firm, subsequently becoming a partner and playing an important role in the business.

Hayward Tyler's imagination and innovation in developing new products was matched by its readiness to embrace new working practices. A private telephone line between London and Luton was installed in 1890, representing the ultimate in advanced technology.

Hayward Tyler was also one of the first firms in London to install a typewriter, thus becoming one of Remington's oldest customers. The most radical move of all was the appointment of a lady typist to work in the London office!

In 1891, the company purchased land adjoining its existing site and constructed a new iron foundry. By this time the next generation was ready to take its place in the family firm; Henry Fox Howard, Robert's eldest son, was taken into partnership in 1892, and seven years later Eliot's eldest son, Francis Eliot Howard also became a partner. Expansion then continued with the acquisition, in 1900, of the Universal Water Meter Company; with this came a contract from the New River Company of London for making plumbers' fittings. The beginning of the 20th century saw more administrative changes when the company sold its London premises in Whitecross Street to Whitbreads the brewers; the works were not finally closed until 1904. The partnership then set up offices at 99, Queen Victoria Street, becoming a private limited company the following year with Robert Luke Howard as Chairman and Eliot Howard as Secretary.

Top, facing page: A Double Suction Hot Oil Pump for oil refinery duties. *Bottom, facing page:* Gear pump sub assembly. *Above:* The old Machine Shop.

In 1915, a hundred years after the founding of the firm, Robert was succeeded as Chairman by Eliot. Losing his sight during the middle years of his career Robert Luke Howard had headed the company for 60years: he died in 1919 at the age of 85.

In Luton, meanwhile, disaster had struck. When the factory had been under construction many difficulties had been encountered in obtaining the ironwork needed for the frames of the various structures. In the end, timber had to be used instead in many cases, and one of the buildings where timber was used for the roof frame was the large Engineers' Shop. For 30 years this proved perfectly satisfactory, but on the evening of 23rd October, 1903, a spark from a passing train happened to drift in through a louvre in the roof and settle on some wood patterns stored in the East Gallery, which then ignited. Fortunately, some men were working late that evening, and they rang the factory bell to summon the Town Fire Brigade. Unfortunately, despite the best efforts of the Fire Brigade, and the works' own steam pump and fire appliances, it was not possible to extinguish the blaze once it had spread to the roof timbers. Nor was it possible to remove the machinery which stood inside the Engineers' Shop. All that could be done was prevent the fire from spreading to adjoining premises, while inevitably the blazing roof eventually collapsed, causing damage to plant and machinery estimated at £50,000.

The fire was a severe blow to the company, particularly since the loss was by no means covered by insurance. It was also at first seen as potentially disastrous by many of the company's employees, who feared that they would be left, at least temporarily, without a job. In fact the company did all it could to keep the men working. They were all engaged in clearing up the debris and then in setting up temporary working arrangements; as a result the company was able to safeguard the men's pay and keep disruption to its customers to a minimum. One development which was lost forever in the fire however, was an embryonic prototype of the first automobile in Luton; this was still in the early developmental stages when it was destroyed, and the project was never resumed.

The firm's first major innovation as a limited company came in 1908, when one of its employees, W R McDonald, succeeded in insulating an electric motor effectively by winding it with rubber-coated cable, enabling it to be operated under water; this development was incorporated into Hayward Tyler's marine salvage pumps. The Admiralty was the chief customer for these pumps, and some years later they were used to raise the German warships sunk at Scapa Flow during World War One.

During World War Two Hayward Tyler was placed on the 'Admiralty Vital List' and was called upon to manufacture a range of essential components. For a time the company was sole supplier for machined engine fittings and cast engine sumps for Churchill tanks. They were also contracted to provide 75 milling machines for the Ministry of Supply, five steam engines for Admiralty barges, 40 pumps for Operation Pluto, 70 sets of submersible borehole pumps for emergency water supply, and 1,750 small pumps for the No.7 Predictor. During the war, 250,000 Oerlikon and automatic gun parts and breech mechanisms were manufactured onsite. Extra staff were employed on the war work. Fortunately none of those working in the factory during the war was killed, although the company's premises suffered badly, being hit by two bombs during the very first air raid on Luton, on 30th August, 1940, and then further

damaged by land mines in a night raid a fortnight later. The old Brass Foundry Pattern Stores were completely demolished in the first incident, and in the second the Foundry was damaged.

Once the war was over the Company began to reassess its position and look to the future. It planned to increase the output of mineral water machines, and additional premises near Edinburgh were leased for this purpose. The company also arranged a special dinner in December 1946 for its many long-serving employees. Eighty-seven employees and ex-employees gathered together, all of whom had completed at least 45 years' service (who between them had combined experience of almost 4000 years!); the average age of the men was calculated to be over 70.

Meanwhile staff development was high on the Company's list of priorities. A full-time Training or Education Officer was employed, and training programmes were put in place, with all boys who joined the firm straight from school being given the opportunity of organised training.

Top, facing page: *A Glandless Boiler Circulation Pump.*
Bottom, facing page: *Submersible motors on assembly.*
Above: *A Boiler Circulation Pump test loop.*

Their progress was reviewed when they reached the age of 18, and those who showed particular promise were given the chance of becoming student apprentices, which was designed to equip them for an executive post.

The output of the Luton factory was divided into four product groups: oil pumps, Duplex steam and power driven pumps, submersible borehole and de-watering pumps, and machinery for bottling mineral water. Many of the large pumps were destined for use in mines and water supply, and Hayward Tyler was responsible for the manufacture of the world's largest submersible motorised pump at that time, developing 400 horse power and built for export to a mine in Malaya for use in de-watering.

Hayward Tyler has exported in excess of 20,000 centrifugal process pumps to more than 50 countries for many arduous hot and cold oil applications. Another Hayward Tyler innovation was the glandless boiler circulating pump, which is still widely utilised in power generation plants; Hayward Tyler has remained the world's number one supplier of this item and has more recently adapted the pump for the assisted circulation waste heat recovery boiler market.

Hayward Tyler's modern design technology means that pumping and drive systems can be easily adapted to meet individual applications, which include sea water lift and fire-fighting. The year 2008 was a significant milestone for Hayward Tyler, firstly the company celebrated 100 years since developing

that first deep submersible motor, and secondly it built and delivered the largest deep submersible motor in the world, at 3,300 HP, with an operating depth of 4,000ft. The following year saw another milestone passed with the Scottish based Fluid Handling division celebrating 50 years in business.

Primary markets today are Oil & Gas, Power Generation, Renewable Energy and the Chemical Processing industries. Hayward Tyler offers a comprehensive range of fluid filled electric motors and pumps that are designed to meet the most demanding of applications and environments for the global energy markets. In addition, Hayward Tyler provides complete aftermarket services to a diverse industrial market base across the globe, through an integrated support network.

In addition, Hayward Tyler provides complete aftermarket services to a diverse industrial market base across the globe, through an integrated support network. Hayward Tyler offers a comprehensive range of fluid filled electric motors and pumps that are designed to meet the most demanding of applications and environments for the global energy markets.

The company provides mission critical solutions to a wide variety of established and evolving industries, specialising in Oil and Gas and Power Generation but also regularly supplying products and services to the Defence, Chemical, Pharmaceutical, Shipping and Utility industries.

Nuclear Power is an area that is increasingly being spotlighted as the future of cleaner energy, and Hayward Tyler is working closely with customers in this specialised industry building on its large installed base of safety critical pumps, its nuclear accredited facilities and market leading desgns.

Hayward Tyler is also working with some of the most important names in Deep Sea Exploration and Production, helping customers succeed in extracting oil from marginal oil reservoirs in ever deeper waters across the world.

Exceptional build quality is what makes Hayward Tyler products the first choice for so many operators today. Attention to detail and precision engineering is demonstrated at hundreds of locations around the world, with many installations running non-stop for over 20 years.

Industrial processes will continue to evolve and there will always be scope for new specialised power units. Hayward Tyler's innovative approach to problem solving, combined with its vast accumulation of knowledge of pump and motor design, will ensure that it retains its position at the head of this exciting, dynamic and specialised industry.

Today, Hayward Tyler is proud to be a world leader in fluid filled motor and pump technology. The firm is one of a very small number of companies that can trace its history back to the early 1800's and is looking forward with excitement to celebrating its 200-year anniversary in 2015.

*Top, facing page: The winding and test and assembly area. **Bottom, facing page:** Detailed quality inspection inside a motor case. **Above:** A custom designed subsea motor. **Below:** Over the past few decades Hayward Tyler have provided thousands of units for the Petro-chemical industry.*

University of Bedfordshire
A Great Future, A Fascinating Past

The need for vocational training in Luton became more acute when new industries began to find their way into the town in the 1890s, encouraged by the New Industries Committee set up by the Borough and the Chamber of Commerce. The approval of companies such as Vauxhall and SKF brought tremendous new employment opportunities for those with the skills to take advantage of them. Finally, following the Education Act of 1902, Luton was able to take its first step towards the establishment of an institute of professional education with the construction of its 'Secondary school' or 'Modern school', as it was later known, subsequently destined to become the 'Technical College'.

The University of Bedfordshire is based in Luton and Bedford. The University was created by the merger of the University of Luton and the Bedford campus of De Montfort University on 1 August, 2006.

A century ago Luton was a very long way from being a university town. Until the last decade of the 19th century the town's main industry had been the manufacture of straw hats, a trade in which a formal education was widely held to be of no great value. However, there were some, such as hat manufacturer Charles Warren, and F W Beck, a local solicitor and member of the Chamber of Commerce, who felt strongly that Luton should be offering some form of technical and commercial education, and who continued to push for such provision.

Today, the University has two main campuses: Luton (in the town centre) and Bedford (on Polhill Avenue). Both the campuses have on-campus accommodation. There are also two dedicated campuses for the teaching of nursing and midwifery degrees, one at Butterfield Park on the outskirts of Luton, and a second at the Buckinghamshire campus at Oxford

House, in Aylesbury. Elswhere, Putteridge Bury is home of the University of Bedfordshire's Knowledge Hub and Conference Centre.

The University of Luton had its origins in the Modern School first mooted in the 1890s. In the mid-1970s it became Luton College of Higher Education with the merger of Luton College of Technology and Putteridge

Top left: *Luton Modern School in 1908.* *Left:* *The White House, which was built for the Burr family and became the home of the Technical College.* *Above: Early college football team.*

Bury College of Education. With the passing of the Further and Higher Education Act, 1992, the College gained University status in 1993.

In 2005, the University announced that it was purchasing the Bedford campus of De Montfort University. With permission from the Privy Council, the preferred name of the University of Bedfordshire came into effect on 1 August, 2006.

The Bedford campus dates back to the Bedford Training College for Teachers, founded in 1882, and Bedford Physical Training College, founded in 1903. These subsequently merged with a further education college to become the Bedford College of Higher Education.

The higher education areas of the Bedford College merged with De Montfort University (based in Leicester) in 1994. There are currently just under 3,000 students based in Bedford.

Luton Modern School and Technical Institute, the first educational building in Park Square, opened its doors there in 1908.

Amidst many changes the Modern School continued to stand until the 1950s when, along with a jumble of other buildings around it, the past was swept away when Luton College of Technology was built.

On 1 May, 2008, exactly a century after the school opened its doors, academics, historians, former students and members of the local community attended a special ceremony to commemorate its centenary.

*Left: Students driving a custom-built car during rag week in the early 1960s. **Above**: Students enjoying a jam session in 1967. **Below** The Queen visiting the then University of Luton in 1999.*

Putteridge Bury is a neo-Elizabethan country mansion built on the edge of Luton on the A505 road to Hitchin. The campus is situated amidst some thirty acres of landscaped gardens. Putteridge Bury can be traced back to Edward the Confessor's time and has links to the Domesday Book. The building was completed in 1911 and was designed by architects Sir Ernest George and Alfred Yeats in the style of the Prime Minister's country residence, Chequers, having had several redesigns and rebuilds over the years. The campus is today home to the University's Knowledge Hub as well as the University's Conference Centre.

The landmark Park Square building in Luton - the largest campus of the University of Bedfordshire - marked 100 years as an educational site in May 2008.

Park Square played a central part in the history of education in Luton with the University of Luton, Luton High School for Girls, Luton Technical School and Luton Grammar School all starting out in life on the site.

The University's brand new £34m Campus Centre in Luton opened its doors on Monday, 11 October, 2010. Designed with both students and staff in mind, the centre houses a 240-seat lecture theatre, exhibition area for displaying student work and informal learning spaces. It also features the Students' Union, support services and executive offices alongside places to eat – all with an international flavour.

The event saw the unveiling of a painting by local artist Doug Jones which shows the original building as it was in 1908. An official archive was launched where photos and items relating to the building will be formally collected.

The University's Vice Chancellor, Professor Les Ebdon CBE, hosted the reception which included an exhibition of photos, brochures and newspaper cuttings from times past. He said: "Visitors to this site often don't realise that Park Square has a long tradition of education dating back to the 1900s. It's only right that we mark this special anniversary by exhibiting a selection of photos illustrating how Park Square has developed into the thriving campus that it is today."

Meanwhile, between 2006 and 2013, some £180m will have been invested in new facilities.

An £8m Physical Education and Sport Science Centre at Bedford campus would train athletes in the 2012 Olympics. The Bedford campus of the University was selected as an official training site for the 2012 Summer Olympics and Paralympics, and acted as a main hub for other training sites in the Bedford area. The Maldives National Olympic Committee based its

competing athletes at the campus, while Paralympic athletes from Angola, Democratic Republic of the Congo, Ghana, Côte d'Ivoire, Jamaica, Lesotho, Morocco, Pakistan, Senegal, Tunisia, Uganda and Canada were also be based at the Bedford campus. With the exception of Weymouth (host to various sailing events) Bedford accommodated more Olympic teams in 2012 than any other town or borough in the UK.

A £7.8m Learning Resources Centre has also now been developed, as well as a £150,000 annual investment in state-of-

Top left: An aerial view of Putteridge Bury mansion. Set in 30 acres of panoramic gardens it is home to the Knowledge Hub and Conference Centre. ***Top right:*** Future scientists - school children during a visit to the University's science labs. ***Left:*** One of the University's modern lecture rooms. ***Above:*** Double Olympic gold medal winner, Dame Kelly Holmes, opens the University's new student accommodation in Fitzroy Court.

enhance links with businesses and the community. The £1.8 million grant from the Government coming from the HEIF 2 initiative (Higher Education Innovation Fund).

Meanwhile, in Luton, demolition of Europa House was finished in June 2011. Tenders for the construction of a Postgraduate and Continuing Professional Development centre were awarded in the summer and construction started in September 2011. It was scheduled for completion in December 2012. There will then be a commissioning period to move into the £19.3 million new building with an opening date in February 2013.

the-art equipment by the computing department. A multimillion-pound Media Arts Centre has been created, with a further £12m being invested in new facilities in the Computing and Media departments. £1m has been invested in the Luton Halls of Residence, which now provide 24-hour security and a pedestrian entrance overseen by a security guard on duty from dusk until dawn, seven days a week. Students with cars receive a gate swipe-card.

A £34 million redevelopment programme at the Bedford campus has been completed, which now boasts a new £6m Campus

Centre, a £4.5m 280-seat theatre and a £20 million accommodation building, Liberty Park. Elsewhere, £2m was invested on an award-winning site for healthcare students at Butterfield Park, Luton and at Oxford House, Aylesbury. A total of £1.4m has been invested in business facilities, including a new Law Moot Court and unique Business Pods. £700,000 has been invested in laboratories for Psychology, Sport and Exercise Science, and Biomedical and Forensic Sciences.

In less than five years the University has been awarded £4m in Government funding for developing business partnerships and won £20m worth of contracts. It also won the largest solo bid in the country to launch a Knowledge Exchange, to

Today, with £180m invested in facilities, the University has over 25,000 students, with representatives from more than 100 countries. It is home to no fewer than ten research institutes, and makes a £300m annual contribution to the local economy.

From its modest roots over a century ago the University of Bedfordshire boasts not only a fascinating past, but now promises an even more remarkable future.

Top left: Management degree graduates from Vauxhall Motors. *Above left:* The Campus Centre. *Above:* Making huge strides - the new Postgraduate and Continuing Professional Development centre will open in 2013. *Below:* University of Bedfordshire's Luton Campus Centre with café and meeting area.

A M Philpot
Onwards and Upwards

AM Philpot (Hard Chrome) Ltd, today based on Luton's Cradock Road Industrial Estate, has been living up to its motto of 'onwards and upwards' for well over a century.

The business was started in 1902 by Alfred Matthew Philpot (1876 – 1971) after he was asked to leave the Salvation Army Instrument factory because he had been found to have lead poisoning.

Alfred set up his own musical instrument repair business in rented accommodation in Park Street. As motor cars became more common, he was also able to use his skills to repair their lamps and radiators. During the First World War significant business came from the repair to Army staff cars manufactured by Vauxhall Motors.

In 1915, Alfred bought a newly built house in Dunstable Road, where a small workshop was constructed at the far end of the garden to accommodate the expanding business.

Alfred was joined by his son Amos David Philpot in 1919. With the business doing well Alfred purchased some land in 1922 at the back of his home and that of three adjoining neighbours'. This fronted a right of way which later became Grantham Road. Alfred built a further workshop accessed by that right of way.

As brass instruments and car parts often require plating after repair, a decision was taken around 1924 to develop an electroplating department.

The business managed to survive the economic depression of the 1930s, and in 1943 with the help of a Government License a further building was added to the site at Grantham Road. That same year Amos became a formal partner in the family business.

Top left: Alfred Philpot's shop in Park Street, circa 1908. *Left:* A photograph taken in early 1920s of Amos Philpot and his fiancé, Phyllis, who later became his wife. *Above:* A picture taken from outside the factory built in 1922 showing Amos Philpot (top left) and Alfred Philpot (second top left).

In 1949, after the Second World War, Amos's only son, David, joined the firm which now found itself in competition for labour with large companies in the town such as Vauxhall Motors, which snapped up anyone trained in chrome bright-work. Because of this 'Philpot's' decided to focus on hard chrome plating, which they had begun to specialise in to fulfil aircraft requirements in 1941. Over 3,000 Mosquito aircraft had components hard chromed by 'Philpot's' during the war.

Adding a further string to their bow, hard anodising began at 'Philpot's' in 1954, mainly for aircraft undercarriage components for Percival aircraft.

In 1971, Alfred, the company founder died, aged an astounding 95years - despite lead poisoning some 70 years previously. With his death came the end of the instrument repairs business that he had proudly continued, but which was in truth no longer a profit making part of the enterprise despite the high quality.

Amos and his son David now managed and owned the business, but all too soon came a black year for 'Philpot's'.

The radiator part of the business managed to hold its own until in 1985 when its two experienced staff retired and that part of the business became unviable and subsequently closed. Later that same year Amos died aged 82 years, leaving David as the sole family member to run the business. It had relied upon one particular customer's production requirements for hard chrome plating since 1958. Looking after that customer's needs took up most of David's time, leaving only two remaining part-time staff to keep the business going.

These decisions paid dividends, allowing further expansion at Grantham Road in 1959/60. The site had been 'sold' by Alfred to Amos for the reported sum of £1,000, and in 1961 the business was split into its component parts A.M.Philpot (Hard Chrome) Ltd and A.M.Philpot (Radiators) Ltd. It remained a true 'family firm' with Alfred, then aged 85, as sole proprietor of the brass band instrument business, Amos as managing director, and his son David a director, with Amos's wife as company secretary of both companies.

In 1977, at the age of 44 years David had married, but had no children of his own. His wife, however, was a widow with two children.

Top: Alfred Philpot and his grandson David Philpot. **Left and below:** *Two images of Alfred Philpot from the late 1960s which were taken for the local newspaper.*

took a keen interest in the family business. When David retired, it enabled him to indulge in his passion for traction engines, something that had been part of his life since the 1960s.

With the move to Cradock Road came the chance for Andy to offer greater capacity and more efficient production. As more customers were seeking modifications and alterations to components, steps were taken to provide these, as well as the manufacturing of new components from drawings and samples.

The future of the 'family' business was in jeopardy, and David turned to his step son-in-law, Andy Morgan. Andy had served an apprenticeship at SKF Ltd. (the well known bearing manufacturer) as an electrician, but was by that time working for British Telecom on their building services team. He had been maintaining and upgrading much of the equipment at 'Philpot's' over the previous years. David's father Amos had, before his death suggested that Andy might be given the opportunity to join the family business.

Andy took up the challenge, and joined the business in January 1986. From day one he took a fresh look at the way the business was running, and worked hard to diversify and extend the customer base. David backed up all of these changes and suggestions, whilst he did not always agree with them he appreciated Andy's 'business head' and hardworking, hands-on approach.

The steady expansion of the business and staffing levels eventually necessitated a move to larger business premises. Andy, with David's help, bought Unit D Cradock Road Luton, in 1997. David had retired that year but still

In 2006, never one to miss an opportunity or to shy away from taking the occasional risk, Andy added to the business when a local customer went into receivership. Via the Official Receiver the plant and equipment was purchased, enabling diversification into what is now known as the Technical Coatings Division, housed in Milton Keynes.

This complemented the services already available at 'Philpot's' and allowed for another acquisition, taking advantage once again of another customer's misfortune, in this case the business 'acquired' an experienced engineering coordinator, who joined the team with over 20 years experience within the canning industry. The business is now a supplier of two-piece canning components and the associated equipment, in addition to maintaining the core of the business of reconditioning, manufacturing and repair.

Top left: *David Philpot (centre) with one of his traction engines.* **Left and inset** *Philpot's offer conventional turning and milling, predominantly for prototypes, repairs, one-off's and small batch work.* **Above:** *Hard Anodising: the formation of aluminium oxide on the surface of aluminium, which can be electrochemically produced under controlled conditions to provide thick protective coatings with excellent adhesion to the base material and exceptional dielectric strength.*

were already very familiar with the name of the company via motorcycle magazines and journal articles over a number of years. As Andy remains a motorcycle enthusiast himself it is safe to say, 'Philpot's' hopes to be regular stand holders at this event.

By mid-2012 'Philpot's' was employing 23 staff across the two sites, and are providing two apprenticeships over the next two years for individuals willing to learn quality and traditional skills from the firm's experienced and knowledgeable longstanding staff members. David Philpot, who remains fit and well (and devoted to his traction engines), was delighted to hear that the history of the family business is to be included in this book about Luton. 'Philpot's' is now one of the very few remaining engineering firms that has been present and thriving in Luton for over a century.

Since 2008 the business has continued to expand, with a steady increase in turnover despite a difficult economic climate. As a result the company has continued to invest in its staff and in its plant without losing sight of the need to provide a quality service to its customers.

At 'Philpot's' Andy Morgan remains firmly at the helm, but there has been a need to put in place a line management structure to enable and ensure efficient progressing of each job as it makes its way through any number of required processes. These changes have ensured that 'Philpot's' is not only a competitive business, but is prepared for the next stage of its growth.

As Andy says: "Onwards and upwards".

In January 2012 'Philpot's' took on a Project Manager, part of his role includes Health and Safety, ensuring a safe working environment. Taking advantage of his enthusiasm and background in Industrial Science, this new team member has also been tasked with addressing the Green credentials of the business, and there is now an active and robust green and recycling policy, as well as an in-house programme for ensuring mandatory Health and Safety training.

Top left: CNC Universal Grinding Machines: these machines are used mainly for volume production work to meet the rigorous demands and exacting requirements of high production grinding. Above left: Metal spraying service at Philpot's Technical Coatings Division. Below: Philpot's Unit D, Cradock Road Industrial Estate premises.

For more information on A M Philpot (Hard Chrome) Ltd visit www.amphardchrome.co.uk

Another first for the company in 2012 was its presence at the Stafford Classic Motorcycle Show, where regular customers were pleased to be able to bring their pitted motorcycle forks for reconditioning, and to be able to put names to faces, especially Andy's and Works Manager Martin Reynolds'. The two day show attracted a number of new customers, although many visitors

ACKNOWLEDGMENTS

The publishers would like to sincerely thank a number of individuals and organisations

for their help and contribution to this publication.

Bedfordshire and Luton Archives and Records Service

Bedfordshire Police (Mr Ian Hebden)

Getty Images

Mr Pete Hackney

Mr Tony Clarke

Mr Len Midgham